OPPOSING
VIEWPOINTS®
SERIES

| Tax Reform

Other Books of Related Interest:

Opposing Viewpoints Series
The Federal Budget

At Issue Series
Are America's Wealthy Too Powerful?

Current Controversies Series
Government Corruption

"Congress shall make no law ... abridging the freedom of speech, or of the press."

First Amendment to the US Constitution

The basic foundation of our democracy is the First Amendment guarantee of freedom of expression. The Opposing Viewpoints Series is dedicated to the concept of this basic freedom and the idea that it is more important to practice it than to enshrine it.

OPPOSING VIEWPOINTS® SERIES

| Tax Reform

Noël Merino, Book Editor

GREENHAVEN PRESS
A part of Gale, Cengage Learning

GALE
CENGAGE Learning™

Detroit • New York • San Francisco • New Haven, Conn • Waterville, Maine • London

Christine Nasso, *Publisher*
Elizabeth Des Chenes, *Managing Editor*

© 2011 Greenhaven Press, a part of Gale, Cengage Learning.

Gale and Greenhaven Press are registered trademarks used herein under license.

For more information, contact:
Greenhaven Press
27500 Drake Rd.
Farmington Hills, MI 48331-3535
Or you can visit our Internet site at gale.cengage.com

For product information and technology assistance, contact us at

Gale Customer Support, 1-800-877-4253
For permission to use material from this text or product, submit all requests online at www.cengage.com/permissions

Further permissions questions can be emailed to permissionrequest@cengage.com

Articles in Greenhaven Press anthologies are often edited for length to meet page requirements. In addition, original titles of these works are changed to clearly present the main thesis and to explicitly indicate the author's opinion. Every effort is made to ensure that Greenhaven Press accurately reflects the original intent of the authors. Every effort has been made to trace the owners of copyrighted material.

Cover Image copyright Mehmet Dilsiz/Shutterstock.com.

LIBRARY OF CONGRESS CATALOGING-IN-PUBLICATION DATA

Tax Reform / Noël Merino, book editor.
    p. cm. -- (Opposing viewpoints)
    Includes bibliographical references and index.
    ISBN 978-0-7377-5241-0 (hardcover) -- ISBN 978-0-7377-5242-7 (pbk.)
    1. Taxation--United States--Juvenile literature. I. Merino, Noël.
    HJ2381.T384 2011
    336.2'050973--dc22

                                                                    2010043631

Printed in the United States of America
1 2 3 4 5 6 7 14 13 12 11 10

Contents

Chapter 3: What Particular Taxes Should Be Enacted or Repealed?

Chapter 4: How Should the US Tax System Be Reformed?

Why Consider Opposing Viewpoints?

> "The only way in which a human being can make some approach to knowing the whole of a subject is by hearing what can be said about it by persons of every variety of opinion and studying all modes in which it can be looked at by every character of mind. No wise man ever acquired his wisdom in any mode but this."
>
> John Stuart Mill

In our media-intensive culture it is not difficult to find differing opinions. Thousands of newspapers and magazines and dozens of radio and television talk shows resound with differing points of view. The difficulty lies in deciding which opinion to agree with and which "experts" seem the most credible. The more inundated we become with differing opinions and claims, the more essential it is to hone critical reading and thinking skills to evaluate these ideas. Opposing Viewpoints books address this problem directly by presenting stimulating debates that can be used to enhance and teach these skills. The varied opinions contained in each book examine many different aspects of a single issue. While examining these conveniently edited opposing views, readers can develop critical thinking skills such as the ability to compare and contrast authors' credibility, facts, argumentation styles, use of persuasive techniques, and other stylistic tools. In short, the Opposing Viewpoints Series is an ideal way to attain the higher-level thinking and reading skills so essential in a culture of diverse and contradictory opinions.

In addition to providing a tool for critical thinking, Opposing Viewpoints books challenge readers to question their own strongly held opinions and assumptions. Most people form their opinions on the basis of upbringing, peer pressure, and personal, cultural, or professional bias. By reading carefully balanced opposing views, readers must directly confront new ideas as well as the opinions of those with whom they disagree. This is not to simplistically argue that everyone who reads opposing views will—or should—change his or her opinion. Instead, the series enhances readers' understanding of their own views by encouraging confrontation with opposing ideas. Careful examination of others' views can lead to the readers' understanding of the logical inconsistencies in their own opinions, perspective on why they hold an opinion, and the consideration of the possibility that their opinion requires further evaluation.

Evaluating Other Opinions

To ensure that this type of examination occurs, Opposing Viewpoints books present all types of opinions. Prominent spokespeople on different sides of each issue as well as well-known professionals from many disciplines challenge the reader. An additional goal of the series is to provide a forum for other, less known, or even unpopular viewpoints. The opinion of an ordinary person who has had to make the decision to cut off life support from a terminally ill relative, for example, may be just as valuable and provide just as much insight as a medical ethicist's professional opinion. The editors have two additional purposes in including these less known views. One, the editors encourage readers to respect others' opinions—even when not enhanced by professional credibility. It is only by reading or listening to and objectively evaluating others' ideas that one can determine whether they are worthy of consideration. Two, the inclusion of such viewpoints encourages the important critical thinking skill of objectively evaluating an author's credentials and bias. This evaluation will illuminate an author's reasons for taking a particular stance on an issue and will aid in readers' evaluation of the author's ideas.

It is our hope that these books will give readers a deeper understanding of the issues debated and an appreciation of the complexity of even seemingly simple issues when good and honest people disagree. This awareness is particularly important in a democratic society such as ours in which people enter into public debate to determine the common good. Those with whom one disagrees should not be regarded as enemies but rather as people whose views deserve careful examination and may shed light on one's own.

Thomas Jefferson once said that "difference of opinion leads to inquiry, and inquiry to truth." Jefferson, a broadly educated man, argued that "if a nation expects to be ignorant and free . . . it expects what never was and never will be." As individuals and as a nation, it is imperative that we consider the opinions of others and examine them with skill and discernment. The Opposing Viewpoints Series is intended to help readers achieve this goal.

David L. Bender and Bruno Leone,
Founders

Introduction

"Discussions of major tax reform occur about once every decade."

—American Institute
of Certified Public Accountants,
"Tax Reform Alternatives
for the 21st Century," October 2009

The US tax system has drastically changed during the past several decades. One thing that has not changed over the decades, however, is the perpetual debate about the tax system. Controversies have always existed about the type of taxes collected, the amount of taxes paid, and the way tax revenue is spent. These controversies are alive today and calls for tax reform are rampant. Although there is widespread agreement that some kind of tax reform is needed, there is little agreement about how the US tax system ought to be reformed. Understanding how the current US income tax system evolved can give some context for the reform debate that exists today.

Prior to the American Revolutionary War (1775–1783), the American colonies had various methods for gathering revenue. The southern colonies taxed imports and exports, the middle colonies used property taxes and poll taxes, whereas the New England colonies used real estate and excise taxes. When England imposed a series of taxes on the American colonies, beginning with the Stamp Act in 1765, American resistance to taxes became widespread. The resistance to these taxes imposed on American colonies by the British government reached a fever pitch with a tax on tea created by the Tea Act of 1773, leading to the slogan, "No taxation without representation," referring to the fact that the American colonies did not have a democratic voice in the British government. The outrage over taxation was one of the causes of the American Revolution.

After the Revolutionary War, the US Constitution was adopted in 1789, which gave the federal government the authority to raise taxes. Known as the Taxing and Spending Clause, Article 1, Section 8, Clause 1 of the US Constitution reads:

> The Congress shall have Power To lay and collect Taxes, Duties, Imposts and Excises, to pay the Debts and provide for the common Defence and general Welfare of the United States; but all Duties, Imposts and Excises shall be uniform throughout the United States.

Excise taxes were then collected on a variety of goods. This article required taxes to be apportioned among the states according to population, rather than levied directly on individuals.

The Sixteenth Amendment to the US Constitution, ratified in 1913, gave the federal government the ability to collect taxes directly from individuals, after federal income taxes enacted in the nineteenth century became the source of a legal dispute. The Amendment reads:

> The Congress shall have power to lay and collect taxes on incomes, from whatever source derived, without apportionment among the several States, and without regard to any census or enumeration.

The Sixteenth Amendment solidified the ability of the federal government to collect personal income tax from individuals. It continues to be a source of controversy today.

After the adoption of the Sixteenth Amendment, the Revenue Act of 1913, set tariff duties on a variety of goods at around 26 percent and set income tax for couples earning more than $4,000 a year and single people earning more than $3,000 between 1 and 7 percent of income. Shortly thereafter, the expenses of US involvement in World War I (1914–1918) necessitated more revenue, which resulted in a series of income tax rate hikes culminating in 1918 with the bottom rate at 6 percent and the top rate at 77 percent. Taxes were cut during the economic boom of the 1920s, but were once again raised by the Tax Act of 1932, in response to the Great Depression. The 1935 Social Security Act established several social welfare and social insurance programs, creating the need to collect more revenue through payroll taxes. Increased defense spending during World War II (1939–1945) raised income tax drastically, with the top rate for people with incomes over $1 million at 94 percent.

The Tax Reform Act of 1969 reduced income tax rates for individuals, but inflation in the 1970s increased the tax burden during that era. The Economic Recovery Tax Act of 1981 changed federal income tax policy fundamentally, reducing the top tax bracket to 50 percent. The Tax Reform Act of 1986 further lowered the top tax rate to 28 percent and lowered the top corporate tax rate from 50 to 35 percent. After tax increases for the wealthiest Americans were slightly raised in the early 1990s, tax cuts were implemented at the start of the twenty-first century. The debate about the wisdom of the so-called George W. Bush tax cuts of 2001 and 2003 continues today.

The history of the US federal income tax system illustrates that the US tax system has always been in flux. In *Opposing Viewpoints: Tax Reform*, authors explore issues relating to reforming the US tax system in the following chapters: Is the Current US Tax System Working? Is the Current US Tax System Fair for Rich and Poor? What Particular Taxes Should Be Enacted or Repealed? and How Should the US Tax System Be Reformed? The many viewpoints included in this volume demonstrate the wide disagreement about tax reform that is unlikely to cease anytime soon.

CHAPTER 1

Is the Current US Tax System Working?

Chapter Preface

Opinions about the current US tax system are not in short supply. Some believe that taxes should be collected in a different manner. Most people benefit from at least one government program—paid for by taxes—that they believe should not be cut. There is fairly widespread agreement that the tax system is too complicated, but very little agreement about how to fix it. Many are concerned about the number of people who cheat the system. The one area where there is widespread agreement, however, is with respect to how much federal income tax individuals pay.

According to Gallup[1], in 2010 only 3 percent of Americans polled said that they considered the amount of federal income tax they had to pay to be too low. According to Gallup's research, which goes back a half century, this is the highest percentage of Americans that have ever said this—with 3 percent of Americans believing this in only two other years prior to 2010: 2009 and 2004. In this sense, Americans are in wide agreement that the amount they pay in federal income tax is not too low. Those who agree on this point, however, differ on whether or not they believe the amount they pay in federal income tax is about right or too high. In 2010, 48 percent said their federal income tax was too high, whereas 45 percent said it was about right. This is almost a complete flip of the poll results from 2009, where 46 percent said their federal income tax was too high and 48 percent said it was about right.

Throughout the past several decades, it has consistently been the case that only a tiny percentage of Americans polled have said they pay too little in federal income tax, with the difference split between those who say they pay too much and those who say what they pay is about right. Throughout the twentieth century, since the late 1940s when Gallup started

1. Gallup, "Taxes," 2010. http://www.gallup.com/poll/1714/Taxes.aspx.

polling Americans about their taxes, more Americans have always said that the amount they pay in federal income tax was too high than those who said it was about right. In 2003, for the first time a small poll showed that half of Americans believed what they paid in taxes was about right, whereas just less than half—46 percent—said taxes were too high. A poll later in that year showed the opposite. The only other year when more Americans believed what they paid in taxes was about right than believed that what they paid in taxes was too high was in 2009.

Despite fairly consistent widespread agreement that Americans are not paying too little in taxes, there is a lot of debate about the current tax system. How much Americans should pay is just one debate about the system. Other debates explored in this chapter examine some of the varying opinions about the US tax system.

| "By any measure of benefits received Americans are overtaxed."

Americans Are Overtaxed

Doug Bandow

In the following viewpoint, Doug Bandow argues that Americans pay far too much in taxes and the situation is likely to worsen. Bandow contends that despite how much tax is paid by individuals in the United States, the benefits returned are not evident. Furthermore, Bandow claims that because of the deficit and the likelihood of further government increases in spending, the amount Americans pay in taxes is likely to rise in the future. Bandow is a senior fellow at the Cato Institute, specializing in foreign policy and civil liberties.

As you read, consider the following questions:

1. According to the author, Americans spend what fraction of the year working just to pay taxes?

2. Which state, according to Bandow, has the latest "Tax Freedom Day"—April 27, 2010?

3. Social Security and Medicare have how much money in unfunded future liabilities, according to the author?

Doug Bandow, "Tax Freedom Day: Real or Imagined?" *American Spectator Online*, April 8, 2010. Reproduced by permission.

Americans are about to finish paying taxes this year. Kind of. Tax Freedom Day [the day Americans will have earned enough money to pay all federal, state, and local taxes for the year] comes on April 9 in 2010, but it's an artificial freedom. Massive borrowing this year—the federal deficit is expected to run about $1.6 trillion—guarantees future tax hikes. And just wait until the real cost of health care "reform" kicks in. The sky will be the limit for taxes.

Tax Freedom Day

Not that the president is worried. During a recent question and answer session, a worker at a battery technology firm observed that we were "overtaxed as it is." President Barack Obama appeared to disagree. I say appeared, because after denouncing "misinformation" and "misapprehensions," he spent more than 17 minutes talking about just about every fiscal subject except whether we are overtaxed.

Tax Freedom Day [TFD], when we finally stop paying for government, comes a day later this year than last, but about two weeks earlier than in 2007. We still are devoting more than a third of our lives to working for Uncle Sam, but in relative terms things seem to be a lot better than just a couple years ago.

If only it were so.

The relief is temporary. The Tax Foundation, which measures TFD, points out that "[t]he recession has reduced tax collections even faster than it has reduced income" and that legislators "have enacted large but temporary income tax cuts for 2009 and 2010, just as President [George W.] Bush did in 2008." Moreover, the estate tax and "the so-called PEP and Pease provisions [limitations on personal exemptions and itemized deductions] of the income tax" were repealed in 2010 as part of previous legislation.

The Services Received from Taxes

Even as it is, Americans this year will spend more on taxes than on clothing, food, and shelter combined. Obviously, we sometimes make bad purchases. Some of the clothes we wore fell out of style and some of the meals we ate were tasteless. Some of the houses we lived in proved hard to sell.

But consider the value of the government "services" that we received: bailouts of banks, companies, homeowners, labor unions, and most everyone else with political connections; a coming federal takeover of the health care system, which will reduce both the choice and quality of care; a gaggle of foreign "welfare queens" on the American military dole, dedicated to doing as little as possible for their own defense; expanding government bureaucracies at home determined to micro manage our lives at work, at play, and at home; out-of-control entitlement programs set to wreck federal finances; and thousands of pork barrel projects designed to reelect the very politicians who voted for all of the aforementioned programs and policies.

In fact, one has to wonder if Washington can get anything right. Last year Congress passed with great fanfare a "stimulus" bill. Assume the best case analysis, that dumping more cash in social programs, tossing money at infrastructure projects, and subsidizing states and special interests alike can generate job growth. The benefits still would be only temporary, and overshadowed by the long-term cost of the added borrowing.

In fact, the CBO [Congressional Budget Office] predicted that the added spending would increase the GDP [gross domestic product] a little through 2012. Then there would be no net impact for a couple of years. And then the misnamed stimulus would *reduce* economic activity starting around 2015. The best case would be a continuing economic boost through 2014. But in any case the "stimulus" bill would end up cutting the GDP permanently. Which means workers will be receiving lower pay even as they are being forced to pay back Uncle Sam's loans. Heckuva job, Barack!

The president might not get it, but by any measure of benefits received Americans are overtaxed.

The Burden of State and Federal Taxes

The average TFD is bad enough. Many states are worse. Connecticut continues to dominate the number one position, coming in at April 27. New Jersey is number two, with its people paying for government until April 25. New York suffers at number three, with its TFD on April 23.

Happily, a few Americans get off relatively more lightly. At the other end of the spectrum are Alaska and Louisiana, whose residents were able to start partying on March 26. Mississippi was next at March 28.

Unfortunately for all Americans, TFD today is merely the proverbial calm before the storm. In a world of endless red ink and the coming debt tsunami, spending rather than taxing is the true measure of government's burden.

Explains the Tax Foundation: "Since 2008, however, deficits have been massive by any measure, and as a result Tax Freedom Day may give the impression that the burden of government is smaller than it really is. If the federal government were planning to collect enough in taxes during 2010 to finance all of its spending, it would have to collect about $1.3 trillion more, and Tax Freedom Day would arrive on May 17 instead of April 9—adding an additional 38 days of work to the nation's work for government."

This number is striking. The previous TFD record was May 1 in 2000. And that year borrowing would not have pushed the date forward even one hour. In 2000 Washington ran a $236 billion *surplus*, the largest ever. May 1 really did reflect the burden of government.

Future Spending and Debt

And the future looks bleak. In its analysis of the president's budget, released in March [2010], the Congressional Budget Office figured that the deficit for this year would be slightly less than the administration projected, but the collective red ink from 2011 and 2020 would be $1.2 trillion greater, for a total of *$9.8 trillion*. The agency warned that deficits for 2010 and 2011 "would amount to 10.3 percent and 8.9 percent of gross domestic product (GDP), respectively. By comparison, the deficit in 2009 totaled 9.9 percent of GDP."

Then there would be a short drop, but only short drop. Explained CBO: "the deficit under the President's proposals would fall to about 4 percent of GDP by 2014 but would rise steadily thereafter." The federal debt obviously would rise too. As a result, "Net interest would more than quadruple between 2010 and 2020 in nominal dollars (without an adjustment for inflation); it would swell from 1.4 percent of GDP in 2010 to 4.1 percent in 2020."

These estimates don't include any of the inevitable but un-budgeted future spending increases. The FDIC [Federal Deposit Insurance Corporation] has been closing a record number of banks. The Pension Benefit Guaranty Corporation's fund is running in the red. Fannie Mae [Federal National Mortgage Association] and Freddie Mac [Federal Home Loan Mortgage Corporation] continue to lose money—and the financial hemorrhage will reach flood stage if the commercial real estate market tanks, as is widely expected. Most federal health care "reform" outlays don't kick in until mid-decade.

Then there are Social Security and Medicare, which together have $107 trillion in unfunded liabilities. Contra expectations, Social Security began running a deficit this year. And there's no money in the fraudulent "trust fund" to pay for future benefits.

The Need to Cut Spending

Looking just at the time frame just through 2020, CBO warns: "To keep annual deficits and total federal debt from reaching levels that would substantially harm the economy, lawmakers would have to increase revenues significantly as a percentage of GDP, decrease projected spending sharply, or enact some combination of the two."

Of course, we all know the likelihood of politicians suddenly becoming responsible fiscal stewards. America is starting to look like a bigger version of Greece, only a few years behind.

Even after you've finished paying your taxes this year, it's too soon to celebrate. You really aren't done. And you may never be done.

The president and Congress are attempting to run a welfare state on the cheap. Unfortunately, the bill eventually will come due. And when it does we may be lucky if Tax Freedom Day ever comes again.

| "*People support the abstract idea of spending reductions, but don't like actually cutting specific programs.*"

US Taxes Pay for Programs with Broad Public Support

Michael Linden and Michael Ettlinger

In the following viewpoint, Michael Linden and Michael Ettlinger contend that Americans' opinions about taxes contain a contradiction. Although the surveys they cite show the American public as viewing government spending with disdain, they claim that most Americans do not want any programs cut. The authors suggest that Americans' disdain for paying their taxes comes from a lack of information about the programs that are funded by their taxes. Ettlinger is vice president for economic policy and Linden is associate director for tax and budget policy at the Center for American Progress, a nonprofit policy organization.

As you read, consider the following questions:

1. According to the authors, total federal revenues exceeded what amount in 2009?

Michael Linden and Michael Ettlinger, "Where Does the Money Go?" Center for American Progress, April 15, 2010. www.americanprogress.org. Reproduced by permission.

2. What is the only area of the federal budget that has majority support for reductions, according to Linden and Ettlinger?

3. The authors claim that 60 percent of all federal spending goes to what four areas?

Americans paid a lower share of their national income in taxes in 2009 than at any time since 1950. Thanks to the American Recovery and Reinvestment Act, 98 percent of working families got a tax cut this year. The rich, too, have been treated very kindly by the tax code in recent years. The top marginal tax rate on income is fully half of what it was 30 years ago, and the top rate on capital gains is at its lowest point since 1933.

Americans' Views of Taxes

Yet the sheer size of our country and our economy means that the federal government still collects an awful lot of money in tax revenues. Total federal revenues exceeded $2.1 trillion in 2009, and 2010 collections will be up slightly with the economy recovering. So it seems very reasonable to ask, "What does the government do with all that money?"

Most Americans, unfortunately, don't feel they have a satisfactory answer to this important question. A recent Rasmussen poll asked respondents if they thought that the federal government, "spend[s] taxpayers' money wisely and carefully." A whopping 78 percent said no. So it's not terribly surprising that, even with taxes at historic lows, 62 percent of Americans in a recent *Economist*/YouGov poll said that they would prefer to deal with budget deficits by reducing spending alone rather than increasing any taxes at all. (Although a recent Quinnipiac poll makes it clear that the public is completely comfortable with raising taxes on the very wealthy.)

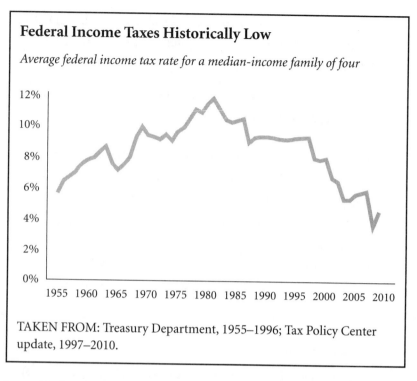

Federal Income Taxes Historically Low

Average federal income tax rate for a median-income family of four

TAKEN FROM: Treasury Department, 1955–1996; Tax Policy Center update, 1997–2010.

The Reluctance to Cut Programs

But, the American public's disdain for "government spending" only holds up in the abstract. The public is much less willing to pull out the hatchet when asked about specific parts of the federal budget. That same *Economist* poll gave respondents a list of budget areas and asked them which ones should be cut. Only one area garnered majority support for reductions— foreign aid. And foreign aid makes up less than 2 percent of the federal budget even using the most expansive definition. Even eliminating it completely would have little discernible impact on the federal bottom line.

There was not even one other area aside from foreign aid where support for cuts cracked 30 percent, let alone 50, including everything from science and technology to aid to the poor. Support for cuts to two of the biggest budget items— Social Security and Medicare—didn't even make it out of the single digits. And lest one think this one poll was an anomaly, recent polls from Quinnipiac and Democracy Corps confirm the overall message: people support the abstract idea of spending reductions, but don't like actually cutting specific programs.

So how is it that the public is so reluctant to axe any specific part of the budget while simultaneously being so distrustful of government spending? We are quick to condemn the government for wasteful spending, but slow to identify wasteful programs. Perhaps one reason for this disconnect is the complexity and opacity of the federal budget. The trillions of dollars spent by the federal government every year go to hundreds of different purposes, from providing health care for veterans to regulating nuclear power, from maintaining highways to patrolling our borders.

Where the Tax Dollars Go

Of course, in a country as large as ours with such a broad array of public needs, it shouldn't come as too much of a surprise that the federal government's activities are just as large and wide-ranging. And just because the federal government does a lot does not mean it does those things poorly. Nevertheless, the sheer number of different ways in which federal dollars are spent can lead to confusion, misunderstanding, and mistrust—something that many conservatives have taken gleeful advantage of.

Getting a better sense for where our dollars go can help take some of the sting out of tax day. Did you know, for example, that more than 60 percent of all federal spending goes to just four areas: Social Security, Medicare, Medicaid, and defense? These are all programs that enjoy broad public support. The next largest category of federal spending is unemployment compensation (5.5 percent). And fewer than 20 percent of people want to cut back there. Another sizable chunk of our tax dollars go to pay for veterans' benefits (3.5 percent), which is the absolute least popular thing to cut according to the *Economist* poll.

Explore the federal budget and see exactly where the tax dollars actually go. It might make mailing in that tax return just a little bit easier.

> "Workers planning to retire in the next 25 years will have fewer opportunities to save and will face a higher tax burden to boot."

American Taxpayers Are Facing a Tax Crisis

Pamela Villarreal and D. Sean Shurtleff

In the following viewpoint, Pamela Villarreal and D. Sean Shurtleff argue that there is a fiscal crisis brewing in America. The authors claim that Baby Boomers retiring between 2011 and 2031 are going to have trouble saving for retirement and higher taxes. The authors cite the Alternative Minimum Tax, projected shortfalls in Medicare, the disappearing George W. Bush tax cuts, and the shrinking Social Security surplus as all contributing to a coming crisis for taxpayers as they prepare for retirement. Villarreal is a senior policy analyst and Shurtleff is a policy analyst with the National Center for Policy Analysis.

As you read, consider the following questions:

1. According to the authors, what is the main problem with the Alternative Minimum Tax, or AMT?

Pamela Villarreal and D. Sean Shurtleff, "The Coming Tax Tsunami," *National Center for Policy Analysis Brief Analysis no. 600*, October 29, 2007. Reproduced by permission.

2. Villarreal and Shurtleff claim that the projected shortfall in all parts of Medicare will require a tax increase of what percentage by 2030?

3. In what year are Social Security expenditures projected to exceed dedicated revenues, according to the authors?

Over the next 25 years American taxpayers will face a fiscal tsunami. The first of the baby boomers will be eligible for early retirement beginning next year [2008] and will be eligible for Medicare in 2011. The last of the Baby Boom generation, born in 1964, will reach normal retirement age (67 years) in 2031. Most baby boomers are approaching their peak earning years when they have the greatest capacity to save for retirement. Many failed to save when they were younger and need to catch up. Unfortunately, expected tax increases will make it increasingly difficult for each succeeding age cohort to save for retirement. Following are some of the tax hikes coming down the pike.

The Exploding Alternative Minimum Tax

The idea behind the Alternative Minimum Tax (AMT) was to tax wealthy households who had so many deductions they paid no income tax. The AMT excludes a basic amount of income and imposes AMT rates on income above that amount. Taxpayers must pay what is owed under the standard tax code or under the AMT—whichever is higher. But the income threshold for the AMT was not adjusted for inflation for many years. As a result, the number of people required to pay the AMT grew steadily. The 2001 [George W.] Bush tax cut bill included an AMT inflation adjustment:

- From 2000 to 2005, the AMT income threshold for single filers rose 26 percent, from $33,750 to $42,500.

- The income exclusion for joint filers rose 39 percent, from $45,000 to $62,550.

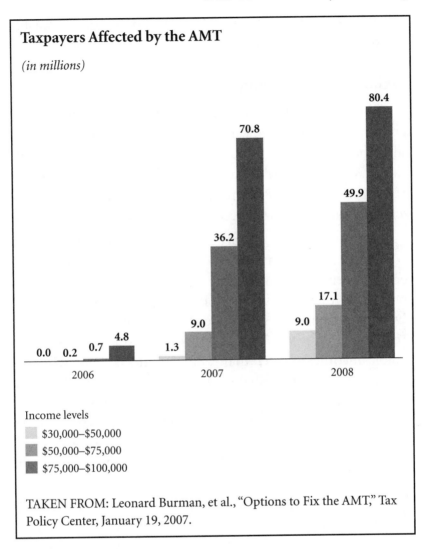

Taxpayers Affected by the AMT

(in millions)

Income levels
- $30,000–$50,000
- $50,000–$75,000
- $75,000–$100,000

TAKEN FROM: Leonard Burman, et al., "Options to Fix the AMT," Tax Policy Center, January 19, 2007.

But these higher income exemptions expire this year. As a result, almost 19 million additional taxpayers earning less than $100,000 will be subject to the AMT, and each will pay on average nearly $3,000 more in taxes on income earned in 2007. Income saved in tax-deferred accounts is excluded from taxable income for AMT calculations. But deposits to after-tax retirement accounts, such as Roth IRAs [individual retirement accounts], are made from disposable income, and boomers with Roth accounts will have $3,000 less, on average, available to save due to their higher tax payments.

Medicare, the Sleeping Giant

Over the past four years, the revenue generated by the 2.9 percent payroll tax for Medicare Part A (Hospital Insurance) has fallen short of outlays. In 2006, this annual deficit reached $10 billion. Moreover, over the next 10 years, Part A expenditures are expected to grow 85 percent to $385 billion, and the projected annual shortfall will grow to nearly $45 billion in 2016.

In addition, Medicare Part B, which covers office visits and physicians' fees, is financed by beneficiaries' premiums and general revenues. Premiums are adjusted periodically to cover about one-fourth of the Part B expenditures while general revenues (income taxes) finance the remaining three-fourths. Premiums are up to 73 percent higher for single seniors with taxable incomes greater than $80,000 and couples with incomes greater than $160,000. These income thresholds have been adjusted annually for inflation. However, President Bush's budget proposal for 2008 calls for eliminating these inflation adjustments. Thus, over the years, as inflation pushes more Medicare beneficiaries above the income thresholds, they will pay higher premiums.

Filling the projected shortfall in all parts of Medicare will require an income tax increase of 22.7 percent by 2030! Thus, younger baby boomers could face a much higher tax burden in their retirement years to pay for their own Medicare benefits.

The Disappearing Bush Tax Cuts

The 2001 and 2003 Bush income tax cuts lowered tax rates throughout the income range and reduced capital gains taxes. But if the provisions are not made permanent, these reduced rates will expire soon:

- In 2009, the tax bracket for the lowest income-earners will rise from 10 percent to 15 percent; the highest earners will face an increase from 35 percent to more than 39 percent.

- In 2011, the capital gains tax rate will increase from 15 percent to 20 percent for most taxpayers, and will increase from 5 percent to 10 percent for taxpayers in the 10 percent and 15 percent federal tax brackets.

- The tax rate for dividends will rise from 15 percent for most taxpayers to normal income tax rates, which can exceed 39 percent!

These tax changes will have a significant impact on retirees and workers approaching retirement. Tax hikes on capital gains and dividends will be especially burdensome on boomers. For instance, the Tax Foundation reports that in 2004:

- The 45-to-54-year-old age group, all of whom are boomers, claimed 22 percent of all dividend income and 22 percent of all capital gains, the highest percentage of dividends and capital gains for any age group.

- Like the cohorts before them, boomers are likely to receive substantial income from capital gains in retirement; in 2004, 30 percent of 65-to-74-year olds claimed capital gains, a higher percentage than any other age group.

- More than half (51 percent) of 65-to-74-year olds reported dividend income, also a higher percentage than any other age group.

In addition to tax increases, if current tax provisions expire, the limit on contributions individuals can make to an IRA will no longer rise by $500 a year and instead will remain at the current level of $4,500 per individual. This means baby boomers will face new limits on their ability to sock away extra savings for retirement and take advantage of catch-up contributions for those over age 50.

Democrats on the House Ways and Means committee have proposed an increase in the top income tax rate from 35 percent to 39.6 percent before 2010, and a gradual rise to 44 percent after that. The measure did not reach the House floor, but it clearly shows support for even more tax increases.

The Incredible Shrinking Social Security Surplus

Currently, the payroll taxes of today's workers pay the Social Security benefits of today's retirees, with a "surplus" left over that is spent on other government programs. In 2017, however, Social Security expenditures are projected to exceed dedicated revenues. By 2020, the deficit will reach almost $68 billion, and will continue to increase thereafter. Closing this growing fiscal gap will require higher taxes or lower-than-projected benefits. According to the 2007 Trustees' Report, an immediate payroll tax increase of almost 16 percent would keep the program solvent through 2075 assuming the revenues are saved and invested. Alternatively, benefits could be immediately reduced 13 percent. Baby boomers, both working and retired, could face both.

Workers planning to retire in the next 25 years will have fewer opportunities to save and will face a higher tax burden to boot. What can be done to avert this impending disaster? The aim should be to maximize the opportunities for baby boomers to earn and save without tax penalties, while restraining spending growth on elderly entitlements. To do so, Congress should:

- Make the Bush tax cuts permanent—particularly the income, dividends and capital gains tax rates.

- Continue to raise the ceiling on retirement account contributions, and retain the higher "catch up" contribution allowed for 50-year-old and older workers.

- To avoid payroll tax increases and slow the growth of Medicare spending, allow workers to contribute after-tax earnings to an account to "prepay" retirement health care expenditures.

- Similarly, allow younger baby boomers to prefund their Social Security benefits by saving some of their payroll taxes in personal retirement accounts, reducing their dependence on the pay-as-you go system.

"We may hate our taxes, but we pay far less than people in other wealthy countries."

There Are Many Myths About the US Tax System

Roberton Williams and Rosanne Altshuler

In the following viewpoint, Roberton Williams and Rosanne Altshuler contend that there are five common myths about the US tax system. The authors dispute the common belief that many Americans pay no taxes and also deny that Americans are overtaxed. Williams and Altshuler claim that higher taxes would not eliminate the deficit. They argue that tax returns are not as complicated as people believe and they also dispute the common view that people should try to get a tax refund at the end of the year. Williams is a senior fellow and Altshuler is director of the Tax Policy Center, a joint venture of the Urban Institute and the Brookings Institution.

As you read, consider the following questions:

1. According to the authors, what percentage of Americans will pay some form of federal tax in 2010?

Roberton Williams and Rosanne Altshuler, "Myths About Your Taxes," *Washington Post*, April 4, 2010, p. B3. Reproduced by permission.

2. What percentage of Americans use the simpler 1040A or 1040EZ tax forms, according to Williams and Altshuler?

3. The authors claim that income tax refunds averaged what amount in 2008?

April is here, which means it's almost time to pony up and render unto Caesar. We've gathered our receipts and other documents, and dragged ourselves to the strip-mall tax preparer or fired up do-it-yourself software to determine how big our refund is—or how much we owe Uncle Sam. No one likes to pay taxes, but as we get ready to stand in line at the post office on the 15th, it might be useful to dispel some of the most common myths about this springtime ritual.

Myth 1: The Poorest and the Richest Americans Pay No Taxes

About 45 percent of households will owe no federal income tax in 2010, according to our estimates. Half of them earn too little, while the other half—mostly middle- and lower-income households—will take advantage of tax credits such as the earned income credit, the child and child-care credits, the American Opportunity and Lifetime Learning credits, which help pay for college, and the saver's credit, which subsidizes retirement saving.

But even citizens who pay no income tax still pay other kinds of taxes. They pay Social Security and Medicare taxes when they work, sales taxes when they buy things and property taxes on their homes. Drivers pay gasoline taxes, and smokers and drinkers pay excise taxes on tobacco and alcohol. According to our research, more than 75 percent of us will pay at least some form of federal tax in 2010.

Those who pay no federal taxes are mostly the low-income elderly or very poor families with children. Even about half of those with annual incomes under $10,000 pay some federal tax, most often payroll taxes on wages.

And yes, the richest Americans pay taxes, too. Though a tiny minority manage to avoid federal income tax through elaborate tax planning, 99.7 percent of those with annual incomes above $1 million will pay federal taxes this year, surrendering 27 percent of their earnings to the government. The average American taxpayer pays 18 percent.

Myth 2: Americans Are Overtaxed

In 2007, federal, state and local taxes claimed about $3.8 trillion, or 27 percent of U.S. gross domestic product. That's nearly $13,000 for every American. Two-thirds of tax revenues went to the federal government.

It may sound like a lot, but other developed countries collect even more. In 2006, taxes in 30 of the world's richest countries averaged 36 percent of GDP [gross domestic product]; only Mexico, Turkey, South Korea and Japan had tax rates lower than ours. And taxes in many European countries exceeded 40 percent of GDP because these nations offer more extensive government services than the United States does.

Americans do pay far more in individual income taxes than residents of other wealthy nations. Nearly 37 percent of U.S. tax revenue came from personal income taxes in 2006, about 10 percentage points more, on average, than in other industrialized countries. But we pay much less in sales taxes; 17 percent of 2006 U.S. tax receipts were from taxes on goods and services, or about half the 32 percent average for rich countries.

Bottom line: We may hate our taxes, but we pay far less than people in other wealthy countries.

Myth 3: Higher Taxes Could Eliminate the Federal Deficit

Washington spends more than it takes in through tax revenues, resulting in a projected budget deficit of almost $1.35

Reducing the Deficit Through Tax Hikes

None of the options we have examined would provide a realistic approach to reducing the deficit over the coming decade, particularly if we impose our more stringent goal of cutting the deficit to just 2 percent of GDP [gross domestic product]. That goal would require tax increases that would cut after-tax income by an average of just over 2 percent, a politically difficult action. All of the changes we examine would be progressive, imposing greater costs on those higher up the income distribution; some of the options would be significantly more progressive than others. However, the most progressive—raising tax rates only for the wealthiest taxpayers—would require increasing the top tax rate to 56.4 percent under current law and to over 90 percent under the administration baseline [the Barack Obama administration's 2010 baseline that permanently extends some of the George W. Bush tax cuts, among other permanent tax changes]. Because most of the additional tax burden would hit the top end of the income distribution, either situation would impose substantial efficiency costs on the economy, raise less revenue than generated in our simple simulations that ignore behavioral effects, and meet with great political opposition.

Rosanne Altshuler, Katherine Lim and Roberton Williams,
"Desperately Seeking Revenue," Tax Policy Center,
January 29, 2010. www.taxpolicycenter.org.

trillion in 2010, or 9 percent of GDP, according to the Congressional Budget Office. Couldn't we get rid of the deficit by raising taxes?

No. A study we conducted at the Tax Policy Center found that Washington would have to raise taxes by almost 40 percent to reduce—not eliminate, just reduce—the deficit to 3 percent of our GDP, the 2015 goal the [Barack] Obama administration set in its 2011 budget. That tax boost would mean the lowest income tax rate would jump from 10 to nearly 14 percent, and the top rate from 35 to 48 percent.

What if we raised taxes only on families or couples making more than $250,000 a year and on individuals making more than $200,000? The top two income tax rates would have to more than double, with the top rate hitting almost 77 percent, to get the deficit down to 3 percent of GDP. Such dramatic tax increases are politically untenable and still wouldn't come close to eliminating the deficit.

Myth 4: Most People's Tax Returns Are Way Too Complicated

No one claims that our tax system is simple. After all, the Internal Revenue Code runs more than 3 million words, and the instructions for the widely used 1040 form take up more than 100 pages. Small wonder that three out of five tax filers pay someone to prepare their returns, and another one in five uses software.

But most Americans have relatively simple tax returns. Nearly two-thirds of us claim the standard deduction and don't have to itemize our deductible expenses. And 40 percent of us file one of the simpler tax forms: the 1040A or the 1040EZ. The 2009 EZ has just 13 lines. Relatively few of us get income from any source besides wages and salaries, interest, dividends, and pensions, so it's not hard to tally how much we took in.

So why do taxes seem so complicated? Blame Congress. Legislators use the tax code not just to collect revenue but also to encourage and reward specific activities. The 1986 Tax Reform Act greatly simplified the income tax by getting rid of many special provisions and cutting the number of tax brackets. Since then, Congress has expanded the earned income and child-care credits; created the child, saver's, and education credits; established health savings and Roth retirement accounts; imposed different tax rates on dividends; created a class of long-term capital gains with a lower tax rate and doubled the number of tax brackets.

Last year's stimulus bill added temporary tax cuts that benefit house and car buyers, workers, and families with children, but also make tax returns longer and harder to complete.

Myth 5: You Should Aim to Receive a Big Tax Refund

It's wonderful to receive a big check in the mail. And having to write a check to the IRS is never fun. But you're better off owing the government a small amount on April 15 than receiving a huge refund. Here's why: Even though it seems like you pay your income taxes once a year, you actually pay them all year long as your employer withholds taxes from your paycheck. When you file your tax return, you are refunded the difference between the tax you owe and the cash your employer withheld.

Three-quarters of Americans allow their employers to withhold too much; income tax refunds averaged nearly $2,300 in 2008. In effect, we're giving the government an interest-free loan. You'd be better off stashing these withheld wages in an interest-bearing bank account and writing a check to the IRS on April 15.

It's not hard to cut the amount of money withheld from your paycheck. Just give your employer a W-4 form asking to withhold less each payday. Your human resources office should have the form, and it's easy to fill out. But there is a catch: If you owe too much (and there are specific rules defining what "too much" is), you may have to pay a penalty—usually interest on the unpaid tax. And if you're not careful, you may end up owing more in taxes than you saved.

Periodical Bibliography

The following articles have been selected to supplement the diverse views presented in this chapter.

Greg Anrig and
Matt Homer
"Why It's Good to Be Rich—and Getting Better All the Time," Century Foundation, 2008.

Andrew G. Biggs
"Spending, Not Tax Cuts, Is the Real Driver of the Fiscal Mess," *American*, April 16, 2010.

Robert Carroll
"The Economic Cost of High Tax Rates," *Fiscal Fact No. 182*, July 29, 2009.

Mona Charen
"Fair Taxation?" Townhall.com, October 21, 2008.

Citizens for
Tax Justice
"All Americans Pay Taxes," April 15, 2010.

William G. Gale
"The Tax System: Too Complex, Unfair, and Outdated," *Sacramento Bee*, May 15, 2008.

Chuck Marr and
Gillian Brunet
"Federal Income Taxes on Middle-Income Families at Historically Low Levels," Center on Budget and Policy Priorities, April 14, 2010.

Matt Moon
"How Do Americans Feel About Taxes Today?" *Tax Foundation Special Report No. 166*, April 2009. www.taxfoundation.org.

Richard W. Rahn
"Nobody Likes Paying Too Much," *Washington Times*, May 13, 2009.

Robert Stein
"Taxes and the Family," *National Affairs*, Winter 2010.

OPPOSING
VIEWPOINTS®
SERIES

CHAPTER 2

Is the Current US Tax System Fair for Rich and Poor?

Chapter Preface

One of the ongoing debates about the US tax system is whether or not the system is fair among people of different means. In a society where personal wealth and income varies dramatically, the question arises as to what it means for an individual to pay their fair share of the tax burden. Widely opposing views exist as to what kind of tax system is fair. In evaluating these views, it is helpful to understand three different kinds of tax systems: a progressive system, regressive system, and proportional system.

Under a progressive tax system, the tax rate increases as the taxable income amount increases. With respect to federal income tax, this means that individuals with lower incomes pay a lower percentage of their income in taxes, whereas individuals with high incomes pay a higher percentage of their income in taxes. The US federal income tax system has a progressive aspect: the marginal tax rate varies according to taxable income. In 2010, family income up to $16,750 is subject to 10 percent, up to $34,000 subject to 15 percent, and so on, with income over $373,651 being subject to 35 percent. However, with exemptions and deductions factored in, the effective tax rate of an individual is not necessarily progressive with respect to other individuals of different income levels. Proponents of progressive policies assert that it is fair for the wealthy to pay a higher percentage of their income in taxes, whereas those against such policies claim that such a policy violates the principle of equality. Those who advocate a progressive tax system vary in their opinions of how much progressivity in the system is justified.

A regressive tax system is one wherein the tax rate decreases as the amount subject to taxation increases. Billionaire Warren E. Buffett, one of the richest people in the world, has claimed the US tax system is regressive in the sense that middle-class Americans can end up paying a higher percent of income toward taxes than very wealthy Americans. *The Washington Post* reported that at a 2007 fundraiser, Buffett claimed that in 2006, "he was taxed at 17.7 percent on his taxable income of more than $46 million." In that same year, according to Buffet, "His receptionist was taxed at about 30 percent." A tax is said to be regressive if it results in a higher tax rate for those with less income. Proponents of this kind of regressive structure may argue that it is not unfair for people like Buffet to pay a lower percent in taxes since the total tax paid is so much greater.

A proportional tax system is one wherein the tax rate is fixed, rather than varied according to income level. Also known as a flat tax system, the percent of tax paid is fixed for low-income and high-income people alike. Proponents of the flat tax system claim fairness is met by taxing all people at the same proportion, and note that the rich will still pay more under the system. Opponents, however, claim that fairness is not met since 10 percent of income, for example, has so much more value to a lower-income earner than to a higher-income earner.

Underpinning the debate about the fairness of taxes between rich and poor is the core issue of whether a tax system ought to be progressive, regressive, or proportional. This chapter explores some of the widely divergent arguments for fairness under each of these systems.

| *"Taxing the rich may be the only way to make the economic system work for you."*

Taxing the Rich Heavily Is Necessary

Robert Parry

In the following viewpoint, Robert Parry argues that taxes on the rich must be raised. Parry claims that recent changes in the economy have made the rich richer while harming the working and middle classes. He contends that the tax policies implemented under recent Republican presidents have drastically cut taxes for the rich. Parry argues that the populist outrage against taxes on the rich is misguided and that the government must raise taxes on the rich to continue important government programs. Parry is an investigative journalist, founder of the Consortium for Independent Journalism, and coauthor of Neck Deep: The Disastrous Presidency of George W. Bush.

As you read, consider the following questions:

1. According to Parry, the richest .01 percent has increased its collective income by what percentage over the past two decades?

Robert Parry, "To Save the Republic, Tax the Rich," ConsortiumNews.com, July 20, 2009. Reproduced by permission.

2. What specific proposal by then-presidential candidate Barack Obama led to the national stardom of Joe Wurzelbacher, according to the author?

3. The author claims that if the government does not intervene and redistribute the wealth of the ultra-rich, what three types of programs will likely fail?

For all the laid-off "Joe the Plumbers" who share the Right's fury about the "class warfare" of imposing higher taxes on millionaires, there is this hard truth: the rich don't need as many of you as they once did—and taxing the rich may be the only way to make the economic system work for you.

The New Economy

Indeed, the surplus labor of everyone from factory workers to bookkeepers is fast becoming the biggest structural problem facing U.S. society. Even an economic "recovery" is unlikely to put millions of unemployed Americans back to work, at least in any meaningful way.

That's because in today's brave new world of high technology and global commerce, many blue-collar and white-collar jobs can be done more cheaply through computerized automation or by low-cost overseas labor than by American middle-class workers regardless of how much retraining they get.

So, whenever the current recession ends, many Americans who lost their jobs or had to take severe pay cuts are not likely to make up lost ground. Unemployment and underemployment are almost certain to stay high, and those lucky enough to have jobs will have to work harder, faster and longer than before.

Already, most of us scramble to make ends meet, with fewer protections in the work place as unions shrink, with the 40-hour work week disappearing for many, with cell phone and e-mails putting us on call virtually 24/7, and with retirements postponed sometimes indefinitely.

The Age of Technology

This era's great irony may be that those of us who grew up watching "The Jetsons" or similar representations of the future didn't see this bleak future coming. We thought technological progress was going to mean more free time for the human race—to play with the kids, to read a book, to travel or to just take it easy.

Instead, technology has contributed to making our lives more slavish and more brutish, especially when job loss is combined with lost health benefits and endless pressure from bill collectors.

Yet, while the middle- and working-classes have seen the American dream recede, the upper stratum of the super rich have watched the benefits of the high-tech global economy flow disproportionately into their stock portfolios and trust funds, creating wealth disparities not seen in the United States since the age of the robber barons [late 19th century capitalist who gained wealth through exploitation].

The tiny fraction at the top—the richest 0.01 percent—has fattened its collective income by 400 percent, adjusted for inflation, over the past two decades. While this trend was accelerating from 1980 through 2008, the Republican-dominated federal government aided the wealth concentration by cutting income tax rates for the wealthy.

A Change in Taxes for the Rich

Prior to Ronald Reagan's presidency, the top marginal tax rate (the percentage that the richest Americans paid on their top tranche of income) was about 70 percent. By the time, George H.W. Bush left office in 1993, the marginal rate was at 31 percent—and the U.S. budget deficit was exploding.

To get the deficit under control, President Bill Clinton and the Democratic-controlled Congress took the politically dangerous step of raising the top marginal rate to 39.6 percent, a move that contributed to the Republican congressional take-over in 1994.

Still, the Clinton tax hike helped get the federal budget back into balance and led to a projected surplus so large that policymakers fretted about the complications that might result from the U.S. debt being *completely* paid off. However, when George W. Bush took power in 2001, he immediately resumed the Reagan-esque push to reduce taxes, especially on the rich.

Under Bush-43, the top marginal rate was cut to 38.6 percent and then to 35 percent, contributing to another record surge in the federal deficit. By the time Bush left office in 2009, the U.S. government was hurtling toward a $1.2 trillion deficit and the Wall Street financial bubble—inflated in part because of huge bonuses and other compensation—had burst.

The Current Issue of Raising Taxes

Yet, President Barack Obama and the congressional Democrats feared a replay of Election 1994, so they passed a $787 billion stimulus package and implemented costly bailouts for the Wall Street banks without seeking any immediate tax increase. The result has been a further worsening of the federal deficit—and the Republicans accusing the Democrats of fiscal irresponsibility.

Any discussion of raising taxes on the rich—like the House plan to apply a surtax on the wealthy to help pay for health-care reform—brings howls of protest from protectors of the elites. The *Washington Post*'s neoconservative editorial page denounced the surtax as a case of "soak-the-rich."

However, even the *Post*'s editors acknowledged that "a serious case [could] be made that the U.S. income tax system should be more progressive.

"The average rate paid by the top 1 percent of households shrank from 33 percent in 1986 to about 23 percent in 2006.

At the same time, the share of adjusted gross income claimed by that highest-earning sliver of American society doubled, from 11 percent to 22 percent."

Joe the Plumbers

Beyond the predictable defenders of privilege, however, many average Americans still support Reagan-esque tax cuts even when those policies have amounted to "class warfare" against the middle- and working-classes as well as future generations who are getting stuck with the bills.

This is where "Joe the Plumber," a mid-30-ish Ohio man named Joe Wurzelbacher, comes in. Though Wurzelbacher wasn't even a licensed plumber last year, he became Sen. John McCain's symbol of an American everyman, someone whom the 72-year-old McCain called "my role model."

In the closing days of Campaign 2008, Wurzelbacher launched his strange rise to national stardom by chatting along a rope line with Barack Obama about his tax proposals, specifically Obama's plan to lower taxes on middle-class Americans and raise them on people earning more than $250,000.

Wurzelbacher said he was considering buying his boss' company, which he thought might make slightly more than $250,000 and thus might see a rise in taxes under Obama's plan.

Obama responded by noting that any tax increase in that case would be slight and arguing that his tax plan would help America's embattled middle class because it would "spread the wealth." (Later, Obama noted that the vast majority of small businesses don't clear $250,000 and almost no plumbers do.)

Nothing in the Obama-Wurzelbacher exchange was very remarkable. In effect, Obama was reiterating the century-old case for a progressive income tax that assesses higher rates on the well-to-do than on those with modest incomes.

The Charge of Socialism

It was a concept famously advocated by McCain's earlier Republican role model, President Theodore Roosevelt, who in his New Nationalism speech of 1910 sounded far more radical than Barack Obama.

"The really big fortune, the swollen fortune, by the mere fact of its size, acquires qualities which differentiate it in kind as well as in degree from what is possessed by men of relatively small means," Roosevelt said.

"Therefore, I believe in a graduated income tax on big fortunes, and in another tax which is far more easily collected and far more effective, a graduated inheritance tax on big fortunes, properly safeguarded against evasion, and increasing rapidly in amount with the size of the estate."

However, McCain—who apparently had swapped his old role model (Teddy Roosevelt) for his new one (Joe Wurzelbacher)—accused Obama of "socialism" because of Obama's support for rolling back tax cuts for the rich.

McCain's campaign began labeling Obama the "redistributionist-in-chief," a charge that the Democrats finessed during the final days of the campaign but appear to still fear. The Obama administration has shied away from seeking outright repeal of Bush's tax cuts, instead favoring letting some of them just lapse next year [2010].

That reluctance to tackle the issue of tax increases—and Obama's practical political decision during the campaign not to aggressively defend his "spread the wealth" idea—meant that the argument about the need for a greater government role in diverting some wealth from the top downward has been deferred.

An Important Debate

However, it may be the most important debate for the future of the United States and the health of the American Republic. If the government doesn't intervene through its taxing authority to redistribute some wealth that now is concentrating among the ultra-rich, programs aimed at protecting the environment, improving education and providing health care likely will fail.

The American public already is resisting the idea of expanding the federal debt, which translates into passing on the bills to future generations. Obama also has promised not to raise taxes on hard-pressed, middle-income families.

The only other choices are to delay urgent action on the environment, education and health care or to raise tax rates on the rich, the likes of those Goldman Sachs employees who—after the bank benefited from federal bailouts—are expecting $900,000 in *average* compensation this year.

The Government as the Solution

However, beyond the populist outrage over the size of Wall Street bonuses and other excesses of the super-rich is the simple logic that the federal government is the only entity big enough—and the tax structure the only means powerful enough—to divert some of the wealth at the top downward to pay for needed programs and to create needed jobs.

Government spending also is the only practical way to redistribute the extraordinary wealth created by technological productivity and global trade so those twin developments can benefit the broader population and keep the economic wheels spinning.

This spending could focus on pressing needs, like renewable energy, public transportation, improved education and accessible health care. But of equal importance, it could provide today's "surplus workers" with meaningful work so they can pay their bills and support their families.

A more equitable distribution of wealth could benefit the Republic, too, since politicians might be less enthralled to big contributors and big business.

As [Supreme Court] Justice Louis D. Brandeis noted more than 60 years ago, "we can have democracy in this country, or we can have great wealth concentrated in the hands of a few, but we can't have both."

But first the American people will have to decisively reject another famous quote, Ronald Reagan's paradigm that "government is not the solution to our problem; government is the problem."

The public will have to recognize that sometimes the government can be a necessary part of the solution.

| *"The many arguments used by propo-
nents of higher taxes ignore basic economic facts and distort the positive
benefits of the 2001 and 2003 tax cuts."*

Taxing the Rich Heavily
Is Not Good Policy

Curtis S. Dubay

*In the following viewpoint, Curtis S. Dubay argues that taxes
should not be raised on the rich. Dubay contends that raising
taxes on the rich will actually hurt, rather than help, the
economy. Despite the common belief that the rich do not pay
enough, Dubay claims that the rich pay more than their fair
share of taxes already. He argues that the tax cuts of 2001 and
2003 helped the economy and should be continued. Dubay is a
senior policy analyst at the Heritage Foundation, where he specializes in tax issues.*

As you read, consider the following questions:

1. According to Dubay, President Barack Obama plans to
   raise the income tax rate on the highest earners to what
   percentage?

Curtis S. Dubay, "Seven Myths About Taxing the Rich," *Backgrounder No. 2306*, August
3, 2009. Reproduced by permission.

2. According to the author, the top 20 percent of income earners paid what percentage of income taxes in 2006?

3. The 2001 tax cuts increased the Child Tax Credit by what amount, according to the author?

President Barack Obama plans to raise the top two income tax rates from their current 33 and 35 percent levels to 36 and 39.6 percent, respectively. This would undo the 2001 and 2003 tax cuts for Americans earning more than $250,000 ($200,000 for singles) and return the top rates to the levels of 1993 to 2000 during the [Bill] Clinton Administration.

Proposals to Tax the Rich

In addition to these tax hikes, the House of Representatives' Ways and Means Committee, led by Chairman Charlie Rangel (D-NY), favors another tax to fund the government takeover of the health care system. The "Rangel plan" would levy a 1 percent surtax for married couples earning between $350,000 and $500,000 a year, a 1.5 percent surtax on couple incomes between $500,000 and $1,000,000, and a 5.4 percent surtax for couples earning more than $1,000,000. For singles, the surtax would kick in for earners making more than $280,000 a year, $400,000, and $800,000, respectively. It would be phased in beginning in 2011 and could rise higher in future years if Congress decides it needs more revenue to fund its government-run health care system. Contrary to arguments made by proponents of these tax hikes, tax increases in the early 1990s did not lift the economy to the highs experienced later in the decade.

President Obama's and Chairman Rangel's tax hikes would increase the progressivity of the already highly progressive tax code. High-income earners pay substantially higher tax rates than do lower-income earners. If passed [neither has passed as of August 2010], this increased progressivity will damage economic growth by lowering the incentives to work, save, and invest. This will stifle job creation, further slowing the growth of already stagnant wages.

Those who support this tax increase point to several arguments to boost their case. But when these arguments are scrutinized, it is clear they do not hold up. Tax hikes on the rich will not balance the budget or close deficits. High earners already have a vast majority of the federal income tax burden, and the proposed tax hikes will badly damage the economy at a time when it cannot absorb any new negative shocks.

The President should scrap his plan to hike the top two income tax rates and Chairman Rangel his plan to pile additional tax hikes on high earners. Instead, they should propose to immediately cut spending, including reforming entitlement programs, and extending the 2001 and 2003 tax cuts for all taxpayers. Additionally, they should propose further *cutting* tax rates to help the ailing economy.

What Taxing the Rich Does to the Budget

Myth 1: Raising taxes on the rich will close budget deficits.

Truth: Increasing the progressivity of the income tax code by raising the top two rates will not close the deficit. In fact, it will lead to more revenue volatility, which will lead to larger future deficits.

A progressive income tax system collects increasing amounts of revenue during periods of economic growth and decreasing revenue during downturns. It does so mostly because of the volatility of high earners' incomes. During periods of economic growth, their incomes rise sharply and they pay increasingly higher taxes. But because much of high earners' income stems from volatile sources, such as capital gains, dividends, business income, and bonuses, their incomes fall just as sharply during economic downturns as they rose during good economic times and they have less income to be taxed.

Unless Congress suddenly develops spending restraint, increasing the progressivity of the tax code will only amplify the volatility of revenue fluctuations and increase future deficits. When revenue increases, mostly from high earners, during periods of economic growth, spending would increase because Congress cannot resist spending additional money. But, as history shows, when economic growth slows and revenues fall, Congress does not cut back on its spending largesse. Larger deficits would occur because the gap between spending and revenue would grow compared to previous recessionary periods.

Even if Congress ignores the long-term implications of more volatility and decides to close the deficits by raising taxes instead of borrowing as it is doing currently, it still cannot do it just by taxing more of high earners' income. Congress would have to decide to raise top rates to levels most Americans would consider confiscatory. In 2006, the latest year of available data, there was $2.2 trillion of taxable income for taxpayers earning more than $200,000. Assuming the amount of income at that level is similar this year [2009], Congress would need to tax 80 percent of that income in order to close the projected $1.8 trillion deficit. Tax rates at such levels would significantly decrease economic activity and taxpayers would likely avoid or evade paying them so the revenue gains would likely never materialize.

The Fairness of the Tax System

Myth 2: The rich do not pay their fair share.

Truth: The top 20 percent of income earners pay almost all federal taxes.

The top 20 percent of all income earners pay a substantial majority of all federal taxes. According to the Congressional Budget Office (CBO), in 2006, the latest year of available data, the top 20 percent of income earners paid almost 70 percent of all federal taxes. This share was 4 percent higher than in 2000, before the 2001 and 2003 tax cuts.

When only looking at income taxes, the share of the top 20 percent increases even further. In 2006, the top 20 percent paid 86.3 percent of all income taxes. This was an increase of 6 percent from 2000.

Myth 3: The income tax code favors the rich and well-connected.

Truth: The bottom 50 percent of income earners pay almost no income taxes and the poor and middle-income earners benefit greatly from the tax code.

This widely propagated myth has found its way to the White House Web site's tax page: "For too long, the U.S. tax code has benefited the wealthy and well-connected at the expense of the vast majority of Americans."

As shown in myth number 2, the top 20 percent pay almost 70 percent of all federal taxes and over 86 percent of all income taxes. It is hard to see how the rich benefit from a tax code they pay almost exclusively.

The bottom 40 percent of all income earners benefit greatly from the income tax code. In fact, they actually pay negative income tax rates because refundable credits, such as the Child Tax Credit and the Earned Income Tax Credit (EITC), wipe out their tax liability and pay out more money to them than they ever paid in.

Because of refundable credits, a family of four in the bottom 20 percent of income earners paid an effective income tax rate of -6.6 percent in 2006. As a result, such a family received $1,300 through the tax code. A family of four in the second-lowest 20 percent of income earners paid an effective tax rate of -0.8 percent and received $408 of income through the tax code.

The stimulus bill created a new refundable credit and expanded three others. This will further reduce the income tax burden of low-income earners, to the extent they can pay less, and increase the income they receive through the tax code.

The income tax burden of low-income earners has trended down for years. In 2006, the bottom 50 percent of all income tax filers paid only 2.99 percent of all income taxes. This was down 57 percent from 1980 levels, when the bottom 50 percent paid 7 percent.

Altogether, historical trends and the recent tax policies in the stimulus likely mean that when the data for recent years is released, the bottom 50 percent of all taxpayers will have paid no income taxes whatsoever.

The Ability to Pay

Myth 4: It is all right to raise tax rates on the rich—they can afford it.

Truth: Just because someone can afford to pay higher taxes does not mean he should be forced to do so.

The faulty principle of "ability to pay" holds that those who earn more should pay proportionally more taxes because they can afford to do so. Such thinking can be a slippery slope because, technically, virtually anyone can afford to pay more taxes. The ability-to-pay principle has no grounding in economics, as it relies on a completely subjective judgment of fairness.

The tax code should collect revenue in the least economically damaging way possible. Raising rates on the rich damages economic growth because it reduces the incentives to work, save, invest, and accept economic risk—the ingredients necessary for economic growth.

Raising taxes on the rich hurts workers at all income levels—especially low- and middle-income earners. The rich are the most likely to invest. Their investment allows new businesses to get off the ground or existing businesses to expand. This creates new jobs and raises wages for Americans at all income levels. Taxing more of their income transfers money to

Congress that they could otherwise have invested. This means the economy forgoes new jobs and higher wages that the investment would have created for less effective government spending.

There is a tax code that can collect more from the high earners than from the lower earners without being a barrier to economic growth: Under a flat tax, a taxpayer who earns 100 percent more than another taxpayer pays 100 percent more taxes, but faces no disincentive to earn more since he will pay the same rate on every additional dollar earned.

The Economic Impact of Higher Tax Rates

Myth 5: Higher tax rates in the 1990s did not hurt economic growth, so it is all right to raise them to those levels again.

Truth: High tax rates in the 1990s were a contributing factor to the 2001 recession and returning to those rates will damage the already severely weakened economy.

The economy boomed during the 1990s for a number of reasons. One key factor was an advance in information technology. Computers, cell phones, the Internet, and other technological advances made businesses more efficient. This increased profits and wages and created numerous new jobs.

The 1997 tax cut that lowered tax rates on dividends and capital gains from 28 to 20 percent was also a major factor helping fuel the economic growth of this period. It strengthened the already strong gains from the technology boom. The impressive growth of the S&P 500 index after its passage is testimony to that fact. In the year before the tax cut, the S&P 500 index increased by 22 percent. In the following year, it increased by more than 40 percent.

The economic benefits of the technological advances and lower taxes on investment were strong enough to overcome the negative impact of the higher income tax rates and the economy exhibited impressive growth—initially. Even though the economy overcame high income tax rates temporarily, it was not strong enough to resist their negative pull forever:

> A contributing factor to the 2001 recession was the oppressively high levels of federal tax extracted from the economy. In the 40 years prior to 2000, federal tax receipts averaged about 18.2 percent of gross domestic product (GDP). In 1998 and 1999, the tax share stood at 20.0 percent, and in 2000, it shot up to tie the previous record of 20.9 percent set in 1944.

Taxes were high because the top income tax rates were 39.6 percent and 36 percent—the same rates President Obama and Congress now target.

The economy is in a much more precarious position now than it was in the 1990s. In June 2009 alone the economy lost 467,000 jobs. With no new innovations like those that created economic growth in the 1990s on the horizon to jump-start growth today, the economy simply cannot afford tax policies that will destroy more jobs and make it more difficult for the economy to recover.

The Bush Tax Cuts

Myth 6: The 2001 and 2003 tax cuts did not generate strong economic growth.

Truth: The tax cuts generated strong economic growth.

The 2001 and 2003 tax cuts generated strong economic growth. The 2003 cuts, however, were more effective at creating economic growth because Congress designed them expressly for that purpose. They worked better because they increased the incentives to generate new income by accelerating the phase-in of the 2001 reduction in marginal income tax rates, and by reducing rates on capital gains and dividends, lowering the cost of capital which is critical for economic recovery and growth.

Lower income tax rates generally promote growth, but since the 2001 cuts were phased in over several years, they did

High Tax Rates on the Rich

Ronald Reagan used to say that when you tax something, you get less of it, and when you subsidize something, you get more of it. Politicians actually understand this principle when it suits their purposes. They routinely seek to impose higher taxes on things such as alcohol and tobacco, and they explicitly argue that higher "sin" taxes are necessary to discourage drinking and smoking. . . .

Unfortunately, politicians conveniently forget about economic analysis when they decide they want to tax productive behavior. And just as high "sin" taxes discourage drinking and smoking, high income tax rates discourage work, saving, investment and entrepreneurship.

Daniel J. Mitchell, "This is Fair?" Townhall, April 2009.

not kick in quickly enough to change the behavior of workers, businesses, and investors to help boost the ailing economy, so growth remained sluggish. The 2001 cuts also increased the Child Tax Credit from $500 to $1,000 a child. Although a large tax cut from a revenue perspective, the increase in the Child Tax Credit did nothing to increase growth-promoting incentives. Recognizing that the slow phase-in of rate reductions was not generating economic growth, Congress accelerated the rate reductions to increase the incentives to work, save, and invest during the 2003 cuts.

The 2003 tax cuts also lowered rates on capital gains and dividends, generating strong growth by decreasing the cost of capital, which caused investment to increase. More investment meant that more money was available for start-up capital for new businesses and for existing businesses to expand operations and add new jobs. The rate cuts on capital gains and dividends also unlocked capital trapped in investments that paid lower returns than otherwise could have been earned if the tax did not exist. This generated economic growth by allowing capital to flow freely to its most efficient use.

The increased incentives to save and invest, coupled with an acceleration of the cuts on marginal income tax rates, were a major reason economic growth picked up steam almost immediately after the 2003 tax cuts:

> The passage of [the 2003 tax cuts] started a different story. In the first quarter of that year, real GDP grew at a pedestrian 1.2 percent. In the second quarter, during which [the 2003 cuts were] signed into law, economic growth jumped to 3.5 percent, the fastest growth since the previous decade. In the third quarter, the rate of growth jumped again to an astounding 7.5 percent.

Unfortunately, President Obama and Congress plan to increase the income tax rates and taxes on capital gains and dividends. This would reverse the beneficial effects of the 2001 and 2003 cuts and further slow economic growth during this severe recession.

The Impact on Small Businesses

Myth 7: Raising the top two income tax rates will not negatively impact small businesses because only 2 percent of them pay rates at that level.

Truth: Raising the top two income tax rates will negatively impact almost three-fourths of all economic activity created by small businesses.

Small businesses are a vital component of the economy. They create jobs for millions of Americans and are a major factor driving economic growth.

Evaluating tax policy on the number of small businesses that pay the top two rates is not the proper way to determine the impact of raising those rates. What is important is how much small-business income is subject to the top two rates. This measures the extent to which the top two rates affect the economic activity that small businesses create.

Using this more accurate metric, it is clear that the top two rates have an enormous impact on small businesses. According to the Treasury Department, 72 percent of small business income is subject to those rates.

The amount of small business income subject to the top two rates is high in relation to the number of businesses that pay the rates because these businesses are the most successful. As a result they employ the most people and generate the most economic activity.

Raising rates on these successful businesses would damage the economy at any time, but doing so now will only cost more people their jobs. Highly successful small businesses faced with higher tax rates will cut back on plans to expand, hire fewer workers, and lower wages for current workers at a time when the economy desperately needs them to expand and create more jobs.

Higher rates also discourage would-be entrepreneurs from entering the market. This will negatively affect long-term economic growth because businesses that otherwise would have been created and added jobs to the economy will never get off the starting blocks.

No More Taxes for the Rich

The many arguments used by proponents of higher taxes ignore basic economic facts and distort the positive benefits of the 2001 and 2003 tax cuts.

The truth is that the 2001 and 2003 tax cuts were a major factor behind robust economic growth between 2003 and 2007. Undoing those tax cuts now for any taxpayers would inflict unnecessary damage to a struggling economy and needlessly cost many more Americans their jobs.

Adding additional higher surtaxes on high earners to fund a government takeover of the health care system would only do more damage to the economy and lead to more lost jobs and lower economic growth.

Instead of imposing these economy-injuring tax hikes, Congress should close budget deficits and spur economic growth by:

- Immediately cutting spending, including reforming the Social Security, Medicare, and Medicaid entitlement programs, in order to get long-term budget deficits under control;

- Making the 2001 and 2003 tax cuts permanent for all taxpayers; and

- Further cutting tax rates on workers and investors.

Raising taxes on the rich will hurt the economy at a time when the U.S. can least afford further damage.

| "Policymakers should allow the high-income tax cuts to expire on schedule."

Tax Cuts for the Rich Should End

Chuck Marr and Gillian Brunet

In the following viewpoint, Chuck Marr and Gillian Brunet argue that the tax cuts for the wealthy implemented in 2001 and 2003 should be allowed to expire at the end of 2010, including the tax cuts that apply to small businesses. The authors argue that extending the tax cuts is not a good way to stimulate the economy and that such continued cuts will only increase the deficit. Marr is director of federal tax policy and Brunet is a research assistant in the federal budget and tax division, both at the Center on Budget and Policy Priorities.

As you read, consider the following questions:

1. According to the authors, how much higher will deficits and debt climb during the next ten years if the tax cuts for the rich are extended?

Chuck Marr and Gillian Brunet, "High-Income Tax Cuts Should Expire on Schedule," Center on Budget and Policy Priorities, April 1, 2010. www.cbpp.org. Reproduced by permission.

2. What percentage of taxpayers have business income that is not in the top two tax rates, according to Marr and Brunet?

3. The authors claim that during the 1990s when top tax rates were higher, small business employment rose by how many more jobs per year than between 2001 and 2006 when tax rates were lower?

Allowing the 2001 and 2003 tax cuts for couples making over $250,000 (and singles over $200,000) to expire on schedule on December 31 [2010] represents the best course of action for the budget and the economy. Extending those tax cuts for one or two years, as some have proposed, would be highly ill-advised. It would make it much more likely that Congress would ultimately act to extend the tax cuts indefinitely, increasing deficits and the debt for as far as the eye can see—and thereby adding to the long-term risks that deficits and debt pose to the economy.

Exempting small business income from the scheduled increase in the top tax rates, as some may also propose, would do little for the economy in the short term; only the top 3 percent of people with any business income would benefit. Over the long term, such an exemption would likely *harm* the economy and the budget by encouraging tax avoidance and reducing revenues.

The Best Way to Stimulate the Economy

Some argue that now is not the time to allow the 2001 and 2003 tax cuts for high-income households to expire because the economy is weak. But analysis in a recent Congressional Budget Office (CBO) report decisively refutes this argument. CBO examined 11 options to stimulate growth and job creation and found that extending the 2001 and 2003 tax cuts *in* general came in *last* in effectiveness, well behind measures such as boosting unemployment insurance, providing a tax credit for new hires, extending state fiscal relief, and increasing infrastructure spending.

Furthermore, CBO indicated that extending the tax cuts for *high-income households in particular* would rate even *lower* in effectiveness than extending all of the tax cuts. This is because, as CBO explained, "higher-income households . . . would probably save [rather than spend] a larger fraction of their increase in after-tax income." An economy in a recession or the early stages of a recovery needs more spending, not more saving. That is why putting money into the hands of people who will promptly spend most or all of it, like unemployed workers, is much more effective at spurring economic and job growth than putting money into the hands of high-income people who are likely to save a significant portion of any additional income they receive.

The CBO findings point the way toward sounder alternatives. Policymakers should allow the high-income tax cuts to expire on schedule and use the 2011 proceeds for policies that CBO has found would have a much higher "bang-for-the-buck" in creating jobs and strengthening economic growth, such as extending unemployment benefits and state fiscal relief, increasing infrastructure spending, and a jobs tax credit. Once the economic recovery is secure, the savings from allowing the high-income tax cuts to expire should go entirely for deficit reduction.

Over the long term, allowing the high-income tax cuts to expire on schedule would benefit the economy by making deficits and debt significantly smaller than they otherwise would be. There is a broad consensus among analysts that the large deficits projected for coming decades will reduce economic growth.

Tax Cuts and the Deficit

The country is on an unsustainable fiscal path. CBO estimates that even in the unlikely event that Congress enacts all of the deficit-reduction proposals in the President's fiscal year 2011 budget, the debt will climb to 90 percent of the gross domestic product [GDP] by 2020, and annual deficits will be above 5 percent of GDP (and rising) at that time.

If Congress extends the tax cuts for married filers with incomes above $250,000 and single filers with incomes above $200,000—the top 2 percent of U.S. households—then deficits and debt will be *$826 billion higher* over the next ten years than if it lets them largely expire, as President [Barack] Obama has proposed. Extending the high-income tax cuts would increase deficits by even larger amounts in subsequent decades. Thus, if Congress extends these tax cuts, the nation's fiscal trajectory will be even worse, and the risks to future economic growth consequently will increase.

Some policymakers may propose a blanket one- or two-year extension of all of the 2001 and 2003 tax cuts as a compromise measure. This would be a serious mistake from the standpoint of the budget and the economy.

A one- or two-year extension would merely postpone the critical decision on the ultimate disposition of the high-income tax cuts until the next Congress, when proponents of making those tax cuts permanent are expected to have more votes in support of such a move. Thus, a short-term extension would sharply increase the chances for an *indefinite* extension—which would produce higher deficits as far as the eye can see.

Tax Cuts for Small Businesses

Proponents of extending the high-end tax cuts argue, in part, that allowing them to expire after 2010 would hurt small businesses. If Congress decides not to extend the high-end tax cuts, some of these proponents may seek a special "carve-out" for small business income, under which the top rate on that income would remain at 35 percent when the top rate on ordinary income returns to 39.6 percent.

Such a carve-out would do little to boost economic or job growth. It would, however, encourage substantial tax avoidance and likely carry substantial costs, thereby worsening deficits and debt.

As both the Congressional Budget Office and business trade associations have recently explained, firms will not hire workers or make new investments unless they have—or expect to have—enough customers to justify the increased capacity. Whether a firm's taxes modestly increase or decrease matters much less in this regard than the level of demand for the firm's products or services.

In a recent analysis, CBO noted that some small businesses would profit from an extension of the current top tax rates, but pointedly rejected the argument that Congress should extend these tax cuts to create jobs. CBO explained: "increasing the after-tax income of businesses typically does not create much incentive for them to hire more workers in order to produce more, because production depends principally on their ability to sell their products."

The Definition of Small Business

Most small businesses are just that—small. Their incomes are not high enough to face the top marginal rates. According to the Joint Committee on Taxation, allowing the two top tax rates to return to their pre-2001 levels would have *no impact whatsoever on 97 percent of taxpayers with business income.* Only the top 3 percent of such taxpayers are in the top two brackets.

Those who claim that raising the top rates would seriously harm small businesses also tend to rely on an extremely broad definition of "small business." Because the IRS [Internal Revenue Service] does not publish specific, satisfactory data on the taxes that small businesses pay, analysts are left to examine various sources of business income that individuals receive. Some analysts define *any* taxpayer who shows *any* business income on a tax return—including passive income that very wealthy investors secure—as a small business. Defining small businesses in this manner greatly overstates the actual number of small businesses, particularly among households with very high incomes.

For example, most Americans would not describe the nation's wealthiest 400 individuals, some of whom are billionaires, as small businesses. Yet the "Top 400" have a great deal of money to invest and consequently receive significant business income—which means that they qualify as "small business owners" under the broad definition of the term. According to the IRS, the Top 400 received *nearly $17 billion* in S corporation [corporations that pass income, losses, deductions, and credit to their shareholders for tax purposes] and partnership income in 2007 (the most recent year for which we have these data)—an average of *$83 million* apiece. They would benefit very handsomely if this income were taxed at a lower rate than ordinary income. In addition to the wealthiest 400 taxpayers, the following types of individuals are commonly included in the definition of "small business" used in tax debates:

* partners in very large corporate law firms,

* partners in lucrative medical practices, and

* Wall Street bond traders who receive multi-million dollar bonuses and invest some of their income in investment partnerships.

The commonly used definition of "small business" even includes wealthy executives of the nation's largest corporations and financial institutions who rent out their vacation homes.

The Tax-Compliance Problem

Carving out a lower tax rate for small business income also would give wealthy taxpayers a powerful incentive to reconfigure various business and financial arrangements in order to reclassify regular income as small business income. For example, if "pass-through" income (i.e., income from partnerships, sole proprietorships, and S corporations) qualifies for the lower tax rate, the opportunities for wealthy taxpayers to avoid paying the 39.6 percent top rate will be virtually endless.

Even a carve-out just for active income that high-income individuals receive from S corporations would greatly aggravate tax compliance and tax avoidance problems. The Treasury's Inspector General for Tax Administration, the Joint Committee on Taxation, and the Government Accountability Office (GAO) all have noted that S corporation wage compensation is heavily underreported and, correspondingly, distributions of profits from S corporations—which are not subject to payroll taxes—are overreported. The GAO calculated that in 2003 and 2004, S corporations underreported approximately $23.6 billion in wage compensation to shareholders, "which could result in billions in annual employment tax underpayments."

This current compliance problem flows from the structure of the Medicare tax, which applies to the wages and salaries of S corporation shareholders but *not to the shares of the firm's profits* they receive. This gives shareholders an incentive to convert wages to distributions of firm profits (or to understate their wages and overstate the distribution of profits), since every dollar they receive in distributed profits rather than wages saves them 2.9 cents in Medicare taxes. The recently approved health reform legislation increases the Medicare tax, levying a 3.8 percent rate on income above a threshold of $250,000 for married couples and $200,000 for singles, starting in 2013. The increased rate on income exceeding the threshold will apply to investment income as well as wage income, which will generally reduce the incentive for tax avoidance. However, active S corporation income will continue to be exempt from the Medicare tax, increasing the incentive for shifting to that type of income.

Exempting active S corporation income from the scheduled increase in the top tax rates would *more than double* shareholders' incentive to convert wages into distributions or to misreport wages as pass-through income. Every dollar they received or reported in distributed profits rather than wages would save them not only 3.8 cents in Medicare taxes (starting in 2013) but also 4.6 cents in income tax. Congress, instead of addressing an existing tax-compliance problem, would be making it substantially worse.

Tax Rates and Job Growth

In addition, providing pass-through entities with a lower tax rate ignores the fact that they already enjoy a tax advantage over competitors organized as traditional corporations (known as C corporations): pass-through entities are not subject to the corporate income tax.

Firms often organize themselves as pass-through entities to avoid the corporate tax and reduce their tax liability. They are free to organize, or re-organize, themselves as Schedule C corporations if that becomes more advantageous for them from a tax standpoint.

Finally, history refutes the notion that small businesses would suffer under a 39.6 percent tax rate and need an exemption from it in order to prosper. During the 1990s, when the top tax rates were at the levels to which they are slated to return in 2011, small business employment rose by an average of 2.3 percent—or 756,000 jobs—per year. In contrast, between 2001 and 2006, when tax rates were lower as a result of the 2001 tax law, small business employment rose at only a 1.0 percent annual rate (367,000 jobs per year)—less than half as much. In short, the 1990s tax rates did not deter a robust, job-creating economic expansion, and the lower tax rates after 2001 did not prevent a recovery that proved very disappointing in generating job growth.

> "The evidence shows that all Americans,
> rich and poor, benefited from President
> [George W.] Bush's tax cuts."

Tax Cuts for the Rich Benefit Both Rich and Poor

National Center for Policy Analysis

In the following viewpoint, the National Center for Policy Analysis (NCPA) claims that the rich already pay plenty of taxes, even after the tax cuts under President George W. Bush. The NCPA claims that the 2001 tax cut under Bush actually benefited the poor more than the rich. Furthermore, the author claims that raising taxes on the rich not only hurts the rich, but also makes things worse for the poor. The NCPA concludes that tax cuts for the rich benefit all. The NCPA is a nonprofit, nonpartisan, public policy research organization that promotes private alternatives to government regulation and control.

As you read, consider the following questions:

1. According to the author, the top 1 percent of income earners in America pays what percentage of all income taxes?

National Center for Policy Analysis, *Do the Rich and Businesses Pay Their Fair Share?* Reproduced by permission.

2. The NCPA claims that due to the 2001 Bush tax cut, the top 10 percent of income earners increased their share of federal taxes paid by how much?

3. Antipoverty spending increased by what percentage of spending from 1990 to 2004, according to the author?

Critics of [President George W.] Bush's three tax relief plans charge that only the wealthy benefited from the reductions in marginal tax rates. But is this true? And more broadly, do the wealthiest Americans pay their "fair share" of the tax burden?

The evidence shows that all Americans, rich and poor, benefited from President Bush's tax cuts. The rich saw taxes on their dividends and capital gains reduced (as well as their income taxes), and personal income tax rates were slashed across the board, which encompassed every middle-class taxpayer. Even the poor, who generally do not pay income taxes, were rewarded with a higher Earned Income Tax Credit (EITC) and child tax credits.

Progressivity and the Tax Burden

Our tax system, however, is highly progressive, meaning that as one's income rises, a higher proportion of that income is taxed. Thus, those in the highest tax brackets contribute more to the overall tax burden even though there are far more people in lower tax brackets.

- According to data from the IRS [Internal Revenue Service], the bottom 50 percent of income earners pay approximately 4 percent of income taxes.

- The top 25 percent of income earners pay nearly 83 percent of the income tax burden, and the top 10 percent pay 65 percent.

- The top 1 percent of income earners pay almost 35 percent of all income taxes.

- The top 400 richest Americans paid 1.58 of total income taxes in 2000.

The empirical evidence shows that the wealthiest citizens are also paying an *ever-increasing* proportion of all taxes collected by the federal government. Data from the Congressional Budget Office show not only that taxes on the wealthy have risen over time but that the 2001 Bush tax cut barely kept their share of the tax burden from rising further:

- In 1984, after the [President Ronald] Reagan tax cut had been fully phased in, the bottom quintile (20 percent) of income earners paid an average federal tax rate (individual, payroll, corporate and excise) of 10.2 percent.

- The top quintile of earners paid 24.5 percent and the top 1 percent paid 28.2 percent.

- In 2001, after the first Bush tax cut had taken effect, those in the bottom quintile paid average federal income taxes of 5.4 percent, about half of what they did 20 years ago.

- Those in the top five percent saw a slight decline in their federal tax rate (28.6 percent, down from 29.7 percent).

- The top 1 percent, however, saw their overall federal tax burden *increase* slightly, from 33 to 33.2 percent.

Despite the accusation that it was the very wealthiest who benefited the most from the 2001 tax cut, their federal tax burden stayed level at best and increased at worst. Progressivity in the tax system rose and the wealthy now pay about six times more than the poor.

We can also look at the overall share of federal taxes paid to detect a similar pattern. For example:

- From 1984 to 2001, those in the bottom quintile saw their share of the total tax burden drop from 2.4 percent to 1.1 percent.

- Those in the top quintile saw their share rise from 55.6 percent to 65.3 percent.

- The top 10 percent increased their share from 39.3 percent to 50 percent; the top 5 percent's share rose from 28.2 to 38.5 percent; and those in the top 1 percent saw their share skyrocket from 14.7 percent to 22.7 percent.

Overall, the poor paid about half as much of the federal tax burden in 2001 as they did in 1984, while the rich paid about 50 percent more. Even those in the middle class, often said to be hit hardest by increasing taxes, saw their share decline by about a third.

Raising Taxes on the Rich Is Counterproductive

Despite these figures, many critics of the Bush tax cuts still insist that the rich aren't paying their fair share of taxes, and that marginal tax rates should be increased for those in the highest tax brackets.

Interestingly, though, historical examples show us that when marginal tax rates on the rich are higher than 30 percent, the rich actually pay less of the total tax burden, because they tend to shelter, hide or underreport more of their income to avoid those high rates. Alternately, when taxes are lowered on the rich, their share of the total tax burden climbs. Consider the following evidence from three major tax rate reductions:

Tax Cuts Benefit All?

Popular mythology ... suggests that the 2001 and 2003 tax cuts shifted more of the tax burden toward the poor. While high-income households did save more in actual dollars than low-income households, they did so because low-income households pay so little in income taxes in the first place. The same 1 percent tax cut will save more dollars for a millionaire than it will for a middle-class worker simply because the millionaire paid more taxes before the tax cut.

In 2000, the top 60 percent of taxpayers paid 100 percent of all income taxes. The bottom 40 percent collectively paid no income taxes. Lawmakers writing the 2001 tax cuts faced quite a challenge in giving the bulk of the income tax savings to a population that was already paying no income taxes.

Brian M. Riedl,
"Ten Myths About the Bush Tax Cuts,"
January 29, 2007.

- In the 1920s, the top tax rate fell from 73 percent to 25 percent, but the wealthy went from paying 44.2 percent of the tax burden in 1921 to more than 78 percent in 1928.

- In the 1960s, after JFK [President John F. Kennedy] cut the top tax rate from 91 to 70 percent, those making more than $50,000 saw their share of the tax burden rise from 11.6 to 15.1 percent.

- In the 1980s, after Reagan's "supply-side" tax cuts, the top 1 percent saw their share of the income tax burden climb from 17.6 percent in 1981 to 27.5 percent in 1988.

The Myth of Spending Cuts for the Poor

During the 2005 budget reconciliation debate, critics claimed that Republicans were cutting spending for the poor to pay for tax cuts for the rich; however, the facts simply do not support these overheated claims and the accusation that poor families are shouldering more of the tax burden while receiving less of the spending is empirically false.

- From 1979 through 2003, the total federal tax burden on the highest-earning percentage of Americans—who earn 52 percent of all income—rose from 56 percent to 66 percent of all taxes.

- Their share of individual income taxes jumped from 65 percent to 85 percent.

- On the spending side, antipoverty spending has leaped from 9.1 percent of all federal spending in 1990 to a record 16.3 percent in 2004.

The data clearly show that the tax burden is shifting annually up the income scale while spending continues to move down the scale; the people with the highest incomes are paying more of the tax burden while the poor are receiving more of the spending.

Moreover, the persistent increase in federal antipoverty spending fosters an unhealthy dependence on government, For example:

- From 1990 to 2005, the Medicaid caseload doubled to 55 million participants, meaning that the government increasingly is taking over the health care system from private companies and from community and charitable organizations, thus eroding self-reliance, independence, and local community responsibilities.

- The measure of the effectiveness of government anti-poverty programs is not how many people are trapped into financial dependence on the government, but how many people succeed in freeing themselves from dependence on the government.

Furthermore, the mathematically impossible principle that income tax relief should be concentrated among families who pay no income tax prevents any consideration of legitimate tax relief or tax reform. Additionally, the misperception that higher tax rates induce substantially higher tax revenues among upper-income taxpayers translates into pressures for tax increases that harm economic growth without substantially increasing tax revenues. . . .

President Kennedy once said that a rising tide lifts all boats, and he was right. When the economy grows, rich and poor alike benefit from rising wages, incomes, and productivity. Conversely, stagnation hurts all income classes simultaneously. The evidence from the 1960s through today illustrates that lower tax rates correlate with rising incomes for all sections of the population. Even cuts on capital gains and dividends, often thought to benefit only rich stockholders, allow for greater investment and more job creation, which ultimately helps lower-income Americans. Though the wealthy pay an enormous share of the overall tax burden, tax cuts on their income would not only bring in more revenue, but would help lower-income Americans become more upwardly mobile.

| "A system in which almost half the country pays no income taxes and 40% pay all the income tax has gone too far."

Low-Income Families Pay Too Little in Taxes

Ari Fleischer

In the following viewpoint, Ari Fleischer argues that the current tax system in the United States allows too many people to pay no income tax. He claims that the rich shoulder too much of the tax burden, both in terms of income tax and payroll tax, and that their money is unfairly redistributed to those with lower incomes. Fleischer claims that the system is so out of balance that we are reaching a tipping point where government will not have the tax revenues it needs. Fleischer is a media consultant and the former White House press secretary for President George W. Bush.

As you read, consider the following questions:

1. According to Fleischer, 40 percent of Americans pay what percentage of all income taxes?

Ari Fleischer, "The Taxpaying Minority," *Wall Street Journal*, April 16, 2007, p. A15. Reproduced by permission.

2. Fleischer claims that families and individuals who make less than what amount pay no taxes and are given a government subsidy?

3. The author claims that the top 20% of earners pay what percentage of payroll taxes?

If the tax forms you're filing this year [2007] show Uncle Sam entitled to any income tax, you increasingly stand alone. The income tax system is so bad, and increasingly reliant on a shrinking number of Americans to pay the nation's bills, that 40% of the country's households—more than 44 million adults—pay no income taxes at all. Not a penny.

The Distribution of the Tax Burden

Think of it this way. After dropping off your tax forms at the Post Office, you find 100 people standing on the sidewalk. Forty of them will be excused from paying income taxes thanks to Congress. Twenty of them, the middle class, will pay barely a thing. The 40 people who remain, the upper middle class and the wealthy, will pay nearly all of the income taxes.

Look at that crowd again and find the richest person there. That individual will pay 37% of all the income taxes owed by those 100 people. The 10 richest people in the crowd will pay 71% of the income-tax bill. The 40 most successful people will pay 99% of everyone's income taxes. Yet for some lawmakers in Washington, these taxpayers aren't paying enough. Our tax system comes up short in a lot of areas. It doesn't foster economic growth. It isn't very simple. And it certainly isn't fair. The one place where it does excel is at redistributing income.

According to a recent study by the nonpartisan Congressional Budget Office [CBO], those who make more than $43,200 (the top 40%) pay 99.1% of all income taxes, the taxes that support our troops in Iraq and Afghanistan, and, for example, fund the federal portion of transportation, education, environmental and welfare spending.

Those who made more than $87,300 in 2004, the top 10%, paid 70.8% of all income taxes, an increase from their share of 48.1% in 1979. Think about it. Ten percent pay seven out of every 10 dollars and their share of the burden is rising. And those super-rich one percenters? Their share of the nation's income has risen, but their tax burden has risen even faster.

In 1979, the first year of the study, these affluent individuals made 9.3% of the nation's income and they paid 18.3% of the country's income tax. In 2004, these fortunate few made 16.3% of the nation's income but their share of the income tax burden leaped to 36.7%. Think about that. One percent take in less than 17% of the country's income, but pay almost 37% of the country's income tax.

As for the middle class, CBO reports they make 13.9% of the nation's income and their share of the nation's income tax dropped to 4.7%. In 1979, they made 15.8% of the nation's income and paid 10.7% of the nation's income tax.

The Redistribution of Income

The combination of across the board marginal income tax rate cuts and repeated expansions of the earned income tax credit (EITC) for lower-income Americans has created this situation in which fewer people are responsible for paying more and more of the income tax. When President [George W.] Bush in 2001 cut the lowest tax rate to 10% from 15%, several million additional workers were excused from paying any income tax. Raising top rates, as Presidents George H. W. Bush and Bill Clinton did in 1990 and 1993, also shifted the burden to a smaller group of Americans.

The EITC program redistributes money from those who pay income taxes to 22 million families and individuals with incomes less than $36,348. These workers not only don't have to pay any income tax, they're given a government check as a subsidy to help make ends meet. The EITC is also designed to relieve them of the cost of paying for their share of Social Security and Medicare.

If Republicans, including their presidential candidates, wonder why their calls for tax relief don't resonate like they used to, it's because there aren't that many income taxpayers left. They've been taken off the rolls.

As for the Democrats, they historically have raised taxes and redistributed income as a core philosophy. It doesn't matter to them how much money some people pay—the argument is that the wealthy can always pay more. According to this point of view, it's immaterial that the tax code is highly progressive; it can always be made more progressive. While raising taxes on the few to benefit the many might be a political winner, it's an increasingly risky policy to pursue.

If, as now happens, 60% of the people in our democracy can force 40% to pay the bills, what's to stop 65% from making 35% pay it all? Since no one wants to pay taxes, what's to stop 90% of people in a democracy from making 10% pay it all? Or why not let 99% of the country off the hook, as long as the remaining 1% picks up the tab?

The Tipping Point

The problem is that there is a tipping point after which piling taxes onto the rich will leave the government unable to meet its obligations. And perhaps we're already reaching that point, where most people won't have a serious stake in what the government does because they don't pay for it. They want services and benefits, but they don't pay the price. That's a formula for runaway spending and no accountability. In other words, a system that looks a lot like the one we already have.

This can't last forever. When government revenues derive mostly from the wealthy, the fortunes of a few determine the

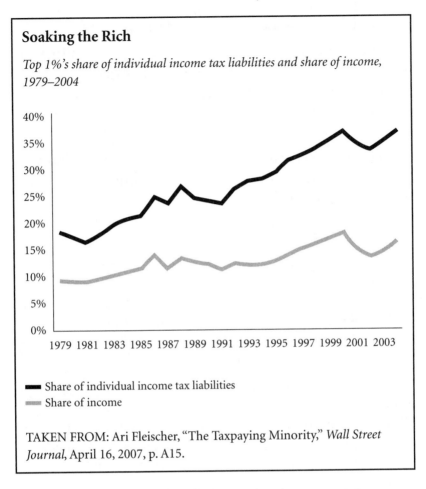

Soaking the Rich

Top 1%'s share of individual income tax liabilities and share of income, 1979–2004

■ Share of individual income tax liabilities
▬ Share of income

TAKEN FROM: Ari Fleischer, "The Taxpaying Minority," *Wall Street Journal*, April 16, 2007, p. A15.

fate of us all. Surpluses and deficits will be driven less by the economic strength of the country, and more by the gains made by the rich in hedge funds, mutual funds, equities and stock options. Like a spinning top that twirls on a narrow point, the top will stay up so long as it continues to go round. Once it slows down it falls, and the government's main source of tax revenue will plunge with it.

What a Catch-22. Members of Congress who want to fund antipoverty programs will have to hope the rich get richer, because the wealthy will need to make more to pay for all the federal programs.

A Good Deal for Low-Income Workers

The usual rebuttal made by those who support raising top rates is that lower income Americans pay Social Security and Medicare taxes and therefore need "relief." Of course they pay these taxes. But then, they alone get a good return on their money.

Top earners, on the other hand, pay payroll taxes so their money can be redistributed to others. According to the CBO study, the top 20% of workers, those with incomes over $64,300, pay 44.2% of the payroll tax while the bottom 20%, those who make less than $17,300, pay 4.2%. In return, when it's time to retire, lower-income workers typically receive more in Social Security benefits than they paid in, while the wealthy, who paid the most in taxes, simply can't live long enough to get back what they paid. For much of the middle class and the wealthy, Social Security isn't a retirement program—it's another program that redistributes their income.

As for Medicare, it doesn't matter that the rich paid far more in taxes; all recipients receive the same benefits. Think of it this way. If Medicare were a car, its price for a low-income worker would be $145 and its price for a millionaire would be $14,500, even though it's the very same car.

Here's why. A taxpayer who makes $1 million a year pays $14,500 in Medicare taxes while a worker who makes $10,000 a year pays $145. But when they retire and visit their doctors or go to the hospital, Medicare reimburses both an equal amount of money. That's a pretty big redistribution of income and a pretty good deal for the low-income worker.

At the end of the day, everyone in this county is in it together. We have an obligation to help the neediest among us and the wealthy should pay more. But a system in which almost half the country pays no income taxes and 40% pay all the income tax has gone too far. Instead of raising taxes and punishing the successful by making them pay even more, it's time to junk the current system and start anew with a code that fosters economic growth for all, not increased redistribution of income for some.

| "The vast majority of Americans are paying taxes in some form."

Low-Income Families Do Not Pay Too Little in Taxes

Leonard E. Burman

In the following viewpoint, Leonard E. Burman argues that the fact that almost half of Americans do not owe income tax is not indicative of an unfair tax system. Burman claims that the Internal Revenue Service (IRS) has taken on the role of delivering needed social programs by offering tax breaks and claims that the fact that about half do not owe income tax is justified, but suggests the IRS could offer more transparency. Burman is the Daniel Patrick Moynihan Professor of Public Affairs in the Maxwell School of Syracuse University and he is an affiliated scholar at the Tax Policy Center.

As you read, consider the following questions:

1. According to Burman, what major change in the tax and transfer system partially explains the statistic that 47% of households do not owe income tax?

Leonard E. Burman, "The Myth of Income Tax Freeloading," Forbes.com, April 15, 2010. Reproduced by permission.

2. The author claims that tax breaks for the richest 1 percent were how many times greater, expressed as a percentage of income, than for low- and middle-income families?

3. What information does Burman suggest that the IRS ought to report back to taxpayers?

This year's [2010] tax season controversy surrounds the Tax Policy Center's estimate that 47% of households do not owe income tax. The estimate has raised concerns about equity (nearly half of families free-riding on the rest of us) and civic responsibility (can democracy work when half of voters get government for free?). It also just ticked off some people who feel they're bearing more than their fair share of the tax burden.

Taxes Americans Pay

The percentage of people who don't owe income tax is especially high for a couple reasons. First, the recession has slashed many families' incomes, cutting their regular tax liability and making them eligible for income supports like the refundable child tax credit and the earned income tax credit (EITC). When the economy recovers, some will reenter the ranks of the taxed. Second, some of the economic stimulus measures, such as the "Making Work Pay" tax credit, were put forward as temporary measures to boost spending. If all the recent tax cuts are allowed to expire, income tax liabilities at the bottom will go up significantly.

Of course, income taxes are only part of the tax burden families face. For most people, Social Security and Medicare payroll taxes are bigger than income taxes. And state and local income, sales and property taxes hit lower-income families hard. The vast majority of Americans are paying taxes in some form.

But the 47% statistic also highlights a major change in our tax and transfer system over the past 30 years: Many social programs that would have been provided by program agencies like the [U.S.] Department of Health and Human Services are now delivered by the IRS [Internal Revenue Service]. Consider that the EITC, the cash-assistance program for working-age families, is about as big as Food Stamps. More families benefit from the child and dependent care tax credit than from Head Start or subsidized child care. More families with children in college are eligible for college tax credits than for subsidized student loans or Pell grants.

Taxes and Transfers

This is not necessarily a bad thing, but it means that income tax filing really combines two functions: taxes and transfers. The Tax Policy Center estimated that before deducting special tax breaks more than 80% of households owe income tax. The one-fifth of households with no tax liabilities are almost all poor (removing them from the income tax rolls was an explicit policy decision of President Reagan in the 1986 tax reform).

That leaves 27% who do not owe income taxes because their subsidies are at least as great as their liability. They are not by any means the greatest beneficiaries of IRS-administered largesse. Tax breaks like the mortgage interest deduction, state and local tax deductions, deduction for charitable contributions and exclusion of contributions to pensions, 401(k) plans and employer-sponsored health insurance are much, much bigger and disproportionately flow to those with higher incomes.

Eric Toder, Chris Geissler and I estimated that those tax breaks—sometimes called "tax expenditures"—were worth 7% to 8% of income for low- and middle-income families in 2007. The biggest beneficiaries, though, were those with high incomes. Tax expenditures for the richest 20% were worth

11% of income. For the highest-income 1%, the subsidies amounted to almost 14% of income.

Given that low-income tax subsidies are raising the reward to work, helping families support children and pay for child-care, and providing assistance with higher education expenses, it's neither surprising nor disturbing that they are significant relative to income (and tax liability).

The Need for Transparency

But I do think there is a problem with the way we account for tax subsidies for people at all income levels. We should break out the tax collection and social program functions of the IRS. It would be a big boost to transparency, might build support for tax reform and might dampen the tiresome rhetoric about tax system freeloaders.

I have a simple proposal: The IRS should report back to taxpayers what they paid in taxes and received in subsidies. (1) How much tax did each family pay in total and as a share of income before considering credits, exclusions and deductions? This would show that the vast majority of working families are shouldering a share of income tax liabilities. (2) What was the value of those credits, exclusions and deductions? This would show that families at all income levels are receiving a lot of welfare through the tax system.

The reports might cause taxpayers to think about whether we could simplify the tax collection and welfare functions of the IRS, which would be very worthwhile. But the fact that low-income families are receiving their fair share of subsidies is a good thing—and especially necessary in these trying economic times.

Periodical Bibliography

The following articles have been selected to supplement the diverse views presented in this chapter.

Arthur C. Brooks   "'Spreading the Wealth' Isn't Fair," *Wall Street Journal*, April 14, 2010.

Economist   "Taxes Are Not Charity," April 8, 2010.

Michael Ettlinger   "Let the Bush Tax Cuts on the Wealthy Expire," Center for American Progress, December 22, 2009.

Nicole Gelinas   "How 'Soaking the Rich' Clobbers You," *New York Post*, April 14, 2010.

Scott A. Hodge   "Why More Americans Pay No Income Tax," CNN.com, April 15, 2010.

Daniel J. Mitchell   "This Is Fair?" *Townhall Magazine*, April 2009.

Stephen Moore   "Reviving Redistributionism," *Wall Street Journal*, July 9, 2008.

Richard W. Rahn   "Confusing Wealth and Income," *Washington Times*, August 27, 2008.

Eric J. Schoenberg   "Raise My Taxes, Please!" Forbes.com, May 21, 2010.

Michael Whalen   "The 'Undertaxed Rich,'" *Washington Times*, March 20, 2010.

OPPOSING
VIEWPOINTS®
SERIES

CHAPTER 3

What Particular Taxes Should Be Enacted or Repealed?

Chapter Preface

The US tax system includes numerous different taxes. Although the federal income tax is probably the most discussed tax in America, there are dozens of other taxes collected from the American people. Most taxes are associated with employment, ownership of property, and the purchase of goods. All have proponents and opponents.

Several types of taxes are associated with employment. The federal income tax makes up a large portion of taxes paid for most people, but many states also have an income tax. All states—except Alaska, Florida, Nevada, South Dakota, Texas, Washington, and Wyoming—impose state income taxes on residents. Payroll taxes are another form of tax that all employed persons must pay. Payroll taxes are deducted directly from income and are used to pay for Social Security and Medicare. Besides the taxes paid by employers for employees, businesses also are subject to taxes on their earnings.

In addition, owning property subjects people to taxes. Both state and local governments often impose taxes on land, homes, and commercial real estate to generate revenue. Ownership of cars and other vehicles also usually subjects one to taxes levied by the state. When real estate investments and other investments such as stock are sold, capital gains taxes must be paid to the federal government on the money gained by such investments. When a person dies, all property, investments, and money may be subject to an estate tax.

Finally, consumption taxes are paid on goods that are sold to and used by individuals and businesses. Excise taxes are paid by the producer, whereas use tax and value-added taxes are collected from the buyer by the retailer.

Some of the primary debates about the current US tax system include whether or not to repeal the alternative minimum tax (AMT), whether or not to enact a value-added tax, and whether or not to keep the estate tax. The AMT is a part of the federal income tax that is an alternative to the regular tax system, originally intended to target wealthy households. A value-added tax is a consumption tax added to a product at each stage of manufacture or distribution. The estate tax, or death tax, is a tax levied on the estates of individuals after death. These are three of the hotly contested types of taxes that either currently exist or are proposed. This chapter examines these and other current debates.

| *"To avert a tax revolt, lawmakers would be wise to take action and repeal this unneeded tax."* |

The Alternative Minimum Tax Should Be Repealed

Chris Edwards

In the following viewpoint, Chris Edwards argues that the alternative minimum tax, or AMT, ought to be repealed and claims that experts agree with him. He claims that the AMT imposes a high cost on taxpayers and thwarts economic growth. In addition, he claims that the tax is unnecessarily complex. Edwards claims that without repeal, this tax will affect millions more Americans in coming years. Edwards is the director of tax policy studies at the Cato Institute and co-author of Global Tax Revolution: The Rise of Tax Competition and the Battle to Defend It.

As you read, consider the following questions:

1. According to Edwards, how many taxpayers paid the AMT in 2006?

Chris Edwards, "The Alternative Minimum Tax: Repeal Not Reform," *Tax & Budget Bulletin*, no. 45, May 2007. Reproduced by permission.

2. The author claims that in 2006 the AMT raised marginal rates on what percentage of taxpayers that would be subject to the tax?

3. Congress has altered the AMT in how many pieces of legislation since 1969, according to the author?

The alternative minimum tax (AMT) is a federal income tax imposed on top of the basic income tax. The two income taxes have different deductions, exemptions, and tax rates. Unlike the basic income tax, the AMT is not indexed for inflation, with the result that its burden is expected to grow rapidly in coming years.

Without relief from Congress, 23 million taxpayers will pay the AMT in 2007. The average liability will be more than $3,000, and that added burden will hit most families by surprise. To avert a tax revolt, lawmakers would be wise to take action and repeal this unneeded tax.*

Tax Experts Favor Repeal

The AMT was enacted in 1969, and the tax has grown steadily ever since. Taxpayers who might owe the tax are required to calculate their basic income tax and then recalculate their liability under the AMT. The AMT disallows certain benefits and uses different exemption amounts. The result is a broader tax base to which the AMT tax rates are applied. If the resulting tax amount is larger than the basic tax, taxpayers pay that higher amount.

Congress enacted the AMT to prevent people from taking too many breaks under the basic income tax. Disallowed breaks include personal exemptions and state and local tax deductions. But since it is Congress that put the special breaks

---

* The AMT has not been repealed as of August 2010, but Congress has passed one-year patches each of the past several years to minimize the impact of the AMT. In 2007, 4.2 million taxpayers were subject to the AMT, according to the Tax Policy Center.

into the tax code, the AMT is really just a Band-Aid to cover up the failure to create a simple and neutral tax base to begin with.

The AMT is not even an effective Band-Aid—it imposes burdens on taxpayers but creates no economic or social value. That's why many experts favor AMT repeal. Groups supporting repeal include the Joint Committee on Taxation, the American Bar Association, the American Institute of Certified Public Accountants, the Tax Executives Institute, the National Taxpayers Union, and the Internal Revenue Service [IRS] national taxpayer advocate. Former IRS taxpayer advocate Val Oveson called the AMT "absolutely, asininely stupid."

High Cost to Taxpayers

In 2006, 4.2 million taxpayers paid about $25 billion in AMT. But if Congress does not extend relief provisions that had been in place in prior years, 23 million taxpayers will have to pay about $73 billion in AMT in 2007. That tax bill, averaging $3,161 per AMT taxpayer, will come on top of the burden of the basic income tax. . . . The average AMT burden will rise to $4,069 by 2012 when it will fall on 38 million taxpayers.

Both middle- and upper-income families will pay the AMT. Married couples with children and those living in high-tax states will be especially burdened. For example, of those earning between $75,000 and $100,000 with two children, 74 percent will be paying AMT by 2010.

Government Does Not Need Added Revenue

The AMT is expected to create large new tax burdens on families, yet the federal government does not need any extra revenue. Federal tax revenues rose 12 percent in fiscal 2006 and are on course to rise 8 percent in fiscal 2007, based on six months of data.

A Miserable Tax (The AMT)

The individual alternative minimum tax (AMT) is a parallel income tax with complicated rules that differ from those of the regular income tax. To compute the AMT, one calculates the regular income tax and then the AMT. If the AMT exceeds the regular income tax, one must pay the government the difference, on top of the normal income tax.

Many people are unaware of the AMT or assume it does not apply to them. Millions have learned otherwise only when their tax-preparation software or paid preparer told them they owed the AMT, or they received an official notice from the IRS dunning them for extra taxes, along with interest and penalty.

IRET Congressional Advisory,
Institute for Research on the Economics of Taxation.
IRET is a nonprofit 501(c)(3) economic policy research
and educational organization devoted to informing
the public about policies that will promote growth and
efficient operation of the market economy.

With all the [President George W.] Bush tax cuts in place, and if the AMT were fully repealed, federal revenues would still be more than 18 percent of gross domestic product [GDP] this year [2007]. That GDP share is the average over recent decades, indicating that there is no shortage of revenues in Washington.

Despite rising revenues, the Bush administration is not leading efforts to repeal the AMT. Instead, it has adopted a position of fixing the AMT on a "revenue-neutral" basis. But that would mean a massive tax increase of about $1 trillion over the next decade, which is the amount of additional revenues the AMT is expected to generate. This position on the

AMT, and the huge spending increases that President Bush has supported, are sadly jeopardizing the income tax cuts that he worked to secure.

Anti-Growth Effects

Some analysts argue that the basic income tax ought to be repealed and the AMT retained because it is more like a flat tax. Actually, it is nothing like the flat tax proposed by [former presidential candidate] Steve Forbes, [former U.S. Representative from Texas] Dick Armey, and others. That flat tax is a simple, consumption-based system that is neutral toward savings and investment. By contrast, the AMT has a punitive treatment of savings and investment and retains all of the income tax system's complex features such as capital gains, depreciation, and complicated rules on personal savings vehicles.

Another growth consideration is the effect of the AMT on marginal tax rates, which influence incentives to engage in productive activities such as working, saving, and investing. It turns out that the AMT raises marginal tax rates on more taxpayers than it cuts them on. In 2006 the AMT raised marginal rates on 71 percent of affected taxpayers, and by 2010 it will raise marginal rates on 89 percent of affected taxpayers.

The Complexity of the AMT

The IRS national taxpayer advocate argues that the AMT is a "poster child for tax-law complexity" and has repeatedly proposed its repeal. The advocate finds that the AMT is too complicated for most taxpayers to calculate and it often surprises families with burdens that they were not expecting and cannot afford to pay.

The taxpayer advocate also notes that most of the tax loopholes that the AMT were originally designed to correct have since been closed, thus leaving no policy purpose for the tax. Yet because Congress has not repealed the tax, millions of families have to spend an average 3.9 hours annually doing

AMT paperwork, according to the IRS. With 23 million people set to pay the AMT in 2007, the total wasted time will be 90 million hours.

The AMT is onerous in other ways. Small and large businesses must perform additional record keeping for items such as depreciation. And the AMT burdens many businesses and individuals who don't currently pay it because they need to perform calculations to see whether they owe it each year.

The AMT burdens the IRS with extra administrative costs, and it bogs down Congress with a recurring tax policy headache. Instead of moving ahead with tax reforms, Congress has spent its time tinkering with the AMT in more than 20 pieces of legislation since 1969. No doubt all those changes have kept tax lobbyists busy as well. The AMT wastes time and effort all around.

The Need for Repeal

Some Democrats in Congress are considering raising AMT tax rates while adjusting AMT exemptions. But that would make the tax even worse and ignore the advice of experts to repeal it. The Bush administration's position of raising other taxes to reform the AMT is also misguided.

Sen. Charles Grassley (R-IA) has the most sensible position on the AMT—full repeal with no revenue offsets. As Grassley noted on the floor of the Senate on April 18 [2007], projected future AMT revenues are "a phony revenue source," and policymakers should not assume that they will receive that money. Rep. Phil English (R-PA) proposes to also repeal the corporate AMT because of its negative effects on manufacturing industries.

Congress passed an AMT repeal in 1999, but that legislation was vetoed by President Bill Clinton. This year, lawmakers have another chance to kill the complex and expensive AMT and make important progress toward tax code reform.

| *"It would be fiscally irresponsible to pro-vide a costly windfall to high-income taxpayers in the form of AMT repeal."*

The Alternative Minimum Tax Should Not Be Repealed

Aviva Aron-Dine

In the following viewpoint, Aviva Aron-Dine argues that the Alternative Minimum Tax, or AMT, ought to be reformed rather than repealed. Aron-Dine claims that despite popular belief, high-income households pay the majority of AMT revenue. She argues that reform is the right way to protect the middle-class from the AMT and claims that the cost of repeal should be off-set. Aron-Dine was a policy analyst at the Center on Budget and Policy Priorities from June 2005 through June 2008 where she specialized in federal tax policy.

As you read, consider the following questions:

1. The author claims that repealing the AMT would cost how much from 2008 to 2017?

Aviva Aron-Dine, "Myths and Realities About the Alternative Minimum Tax," Center on Budget and Policy Priorities, February 14, 2007. www.cbpp.org. Reproduced by permission.

2. According to Aron-Dine, if the 2001 and 2003 tax cuts had not been enacted and without AMT relief, how many taxpayers would pay AMT in 2010?

3. Aron-Dine says the policy of "patching" the AMT with temporary reform will have what annual cost in 2010?

The Alternative Minimum Tax [AMT] was created in 1969 to ensure that the highest-income households could not exploit loopholes, exclusions, and deductions to avoid paying any federal income tax. The AMT acts as a stop-gap tax system, with taxpayers owing their regular income tax or AMT liability, whichever is higher.

Because the AMT parameters were never indexed for inflation, and because the 2001 and 2003 tax cuts substantially lowered taxpayers' liability under the regular income tax without changing the structure of the AMT, the tax will affect a rapidly increasing number of taxpayers in future years in the unlikely event that no changes are made. As a result, there is considerable anxiety surrounding the AMT, and some in Congress are eager to do away with it altogether. Repealing the AMT, however, would cost at least $800 billion over the next decade (2008–2017), and as much as $1.5 trillion, depending on whether the 2001 and 2003 tax cuts are extended (according to estimates by the Urban Institute-Brookings Institution Tax Policy Center). Repeal of the AMT would cost more than repeal of the estate tax.

Public discussion of issues surrounding the AMT suffers from several misconceptions, which seem to be widespread among policymakers and many media outlets.

A High-Income Tax

Myth 1: The AMT is (or is rapidly becoming) a "middle-class" tax.

"What started out as a misguided attempt to tax the 'rich' has become a significant added tax burden on millions of middle-income Americans."—Senator Jon Kyl, May 23, 2005

Reality: The bulk of AMT revenue continues to come from high-income households.

The Urban Institute-Brookings Institution Tax Policy Center estimates that, under current law (that is, in the unlikely event that Congress takes no action to restrict the AMT's reach and the AMT grows to affect tens of millions of additional taxpayers), *more than half* of AMT revenue in 2010 still will come from households with incomes over $200,000 (the highest income 4 percent of all households). About 90 percent of AMT revenue will come from households with incomes above $100,000 (the highest income 16 percent of all households).

It's true that, over time, an increasing percentage of AMT *taxpayers* will be middle- and upper-middle income households. But these households will pay considerably less in AMT *taxes*, on average, than higher income households. In 2010, households with incomes between $50,000 and $100,000 that are on the AMT will pay an average of about $1,000 in AMT taxes, according to the Tax Policy Center estimates, if no AMT relief is provided and the AMT is allowed to swell. AMT taxpayers with incomes between $100,000 and $200,000 will pay an average of about $2,500, while AMT taxpayers with incomes above $200,000 will pay an average of more than $11,000. For this reason, households with incomes below $200,000 will comprise a majority of AMT *taxpayers* but will be the source of less than half of all AMT *revenue*.

Knowing who pays the AMT is necessary to understanding who would benefit from repealing it. Because households with annual incomes above $200,000 are the source of more than half of all AMT revenue, more than half of the benefits of repeal would go to these high-income households.

Furthermore, even assuming Congress does not repeal the AMT, it will almost certainly act to prevent the tax from affecting growing numbers of middle-income households. To date, Congress has provided relief from the AMT in the form of temporary increases in the AMT exemption. If this relief is extended, *nearly all* AMT revenue in 2010 will come from households with incomes above $200,000. Thus, nearly all of the benefits of going beyond the current AMT "patch" and repealing the AMT would go to these very high-income households.

The 2001 and 2003 Tax Cuts

Myth 2: The growth in the AMT was unanticipated and accidental, and so the cost of repeal should not have to be offset.

"It's ridiculous to rely on revenue that was never supposed to be collected in the first place. Another trap is raising taxes to 'pay' for AMT repeal. It's unfair to raise taxes to repeal something with serious unintended consequences like the AMT."—Senator Charles Grassley, January 4, 2007

Reality: Lawmakers put off reform of the AMT so as to use the AMT to mask (and defer) the true costs of the 2001 and 2003 tax cuts. More than half of the current AMT problem is due to the effects of the 2001 and 2003 tax cuts, which pushed millions more taxpayers onto the AMT and more than doubled the amount of tax owed under the AMT in the absence of AMT relief.

The Tax Policy Center estimates that, if the 2001 and 2003 tax cuts had not been enacted, 16 million taxpayers would pay a total of about $43 billion in AMT in 2010, in the absence of AMT relief. With the 2001 and 2003 tax cuts in place, a total of 32 million taxpayers will pay a total of more than $100 billion in AMT in 2010, if AMT relief is not provided.

These effects should come as no surprise to supporters of the 2001 and 2003 tax cuts, who used the AMT to mask the true cost of those tax cuts. In the spring of 2001, when Congressional leaders were formulating their large tax-cut package, they faced a major obstacle. The Congressional Budget Resolution allowed for tax-cut legislation costing up to $1.35 trillion over ten years. The combined cost of all tax cuts on the Administration and the Congressional leadership's agenda, however, was far higher than that. Former Representative Bill Thomas, then Chairman of the House Ways and Means Committee, described the "problem" as a need to get "a pound and a half of sugar into a one-pound bag."

The Congressional leadership accomplished this goal by employing three major gimmicks, all designed to conceal the true long-run cost of their tax package. First, they phased in some of their tax cuts (for example, repeal of the estate tax) over time so that the full costs of these provisions did not show up until the end of the ten-year budget window. Second, they sunsetted all of the tax cuts at the end of 2010, significantly reducing their cost in fiscal year 2011 (the last year of the budget window). Finally, they used the AMT to dramatically reduce the tax cuts' official cost.

The Policy of Patching

As explained above, taxpayers owe the Alternative Minimum Tax whenever their tax liability as calculated under the AMT is higher than their tax liability as calculated under the regular income tax. Therefore, substantially reducing households' tax liability under the regular income tax without changing what they owe under the AMT inevitably increases the number of households that owe the AMT, as well as the amount of revenue the AMT collects. Essentially, if large tax cuts and changes in the AMT are not enacted together, the AMT will take back some (or all) of the tax cuts that households receive under the regular income tax, as households will end up paying tax based on their tax liabilities under the AMT rather than under regular income tax law.

This point is well understood by tax experts, and it was brought to the attention of members of Congress in the spring of 2001, when the Joint Committee on Taxation provided lawmakers with estimates of how the tax cuts then under consideration would impact the AMT. These estimates showed that the new tax cuts would *double* the number of AMT taxpayers by 2010.

Policymakers could have chosen to act on the information the Joint Tax Committee provided, reforming the AMT so that it did not affect rapidly increasing numbers of households and so that households would receive the full value of whatever new tax cuts were enacted. But, because the Congressional Budget Resolution set a limit for the total cost of the 2001 tax cut, providing a meaningful AMT fix would have required scaling back other tax cuts under consideration (such as the large reductions in the top marginal income-tax rates).

Instead, Congress chose to enact a vastly cheaper ($14 billion) three-year AMT "patch" (a temporary increase in the exemption level) in order to maximize the size of the other tax cuts. The patch was enough to make sure that the number of AMT taxpayers did not immediately explode and that most people received the full value of their 2001 tax cuts—but only through 2004.

Had Congress then actually allowed the AMT patch to expire at the end of 2004, the AMT would have taken back a substantial fraction of the 2001 tax cuts in subsequent years. The official cost estimates for the 2001 tax cuts *assumed that this would occur*, and so *they omitted the cost of the portion of the tax cuts that would be taken back by the AMT*. As a result, the tax cuts appeared much cheaper than they otherwise would have.

In reality, however, Congress did not allow the AMT patch to expire, but extended it through the end of 2006 (at a cost of about $80 billion). The Congressional Budget Office now

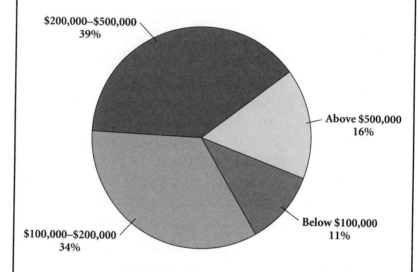

Most AMT Revenue Comes From High-Income Households

Distribution of AMT Tax Revenue Under Current Law By Income Group, 2010

$200,000–$500,000
39%

Above $500,000
16%

Below $100,000
11%

$100,000–$200,000
34%

TAKEN FROM: Aviva Aron-Dine, "Myths and Realities About the Alternative Minimum Tax," Center on Budget and Policy Priorities, February 14, 2007. www.cbpp.org.

estimates that continuing the policy of "patching" the AMT would have an annual cost of about $70 billion by 2010. *More than sixty percent of that cost simply represents the deferred cost of the enacted 2001 and 2003 tax cuts.*

Reform, Not Repeal

Myth 3: The only way to protect middle-class households from the AMT is to repeal it.

"The AMT is a monster that really cannot be improved. It cannot be made to work right. It is time to draw the curtain on this monster."—Senate Finance Committee Chair Max Baucus, January 4, 2007

Reality: The AMT can be reformed—and in a revenue-neutral manner—so as to fully protect middle-class households from the tax.

As noted above, repealing the AMT would cost about $800 billion between 2008 and 2017, if all of the 2001 and 2003 tax cuts were allowed to expire, and $1.5 trillion, if all of these tax cuts were extended (according to estimates by the Tax Policy Center). Over the long run, the revenue losses from AMT repeal dwarf even the cost of estate-tax repeal, another very expensive tax cut that many in Congress have rejected as unaffordable.

Fortunately, various tax experts have suggested reform alternatives that would protect all or nearly all middle- and upper-middle class households from paying the AMT, while preserving the revenue from the tax. More than half of the cost of repealing the AMT would, as described above, go for tax cuts for households with incomes above $200,000. Thus, a fix that better targets relief toward middle-income households would be considerably less expensive than repeal, and its costs could be offset through any number of possible measures.

For example, one approach to AMT reform would be to extend the current AMT "patch" (the temporary higher AMT exemption level that expired at the end of 2006) and index it for inflation. This reform would be better targeted than repeal toward middle-income taxpayers, although at least a fourth of the cost over the next few years still would go to provide tax cuts for households with incomes above $200,000.

Another option would be to simply exempt all households with incomes below a given level (e.g. $200,000) from the AMT. Under such an approach, by definition, *no* household with income below the chosen level would pay the AMT, and the benefits would be targeted to those with incomes below that level.

Either of these approaches would be substantially less costly than repeal, though still expensive. CBO [Congressional

Budget Office] estimates that continuing the current patch through 2017 would cost $569 billion between 2008 and 2017 if the 2001 and 2003 tax cuts are allowed to expire and *more than $1 trillion* if these tax cuts are extended. The cost of an AMT exclusion for households with incomes below a certain level could be less (depending on the income level chosen), but would still be quite high. . . .

Given the range of available options and the grave long-term budget problems the nation faces, it would be fiscally irresponsible to provide a costly windfall to high-income taxpayers in the form of AMT repeal. Rather, if policymakers wish to address the AMT issue, they should enact an AMT *reform* plan that effectively targets relief to middle-class taxpayers and fully pays for the change in a progressive manner.

| *"Introduce a VAT—which, though imperfect, would do less economic harm than an equivalent rise in income taxes."*

A Value-Added Tax Is Necessary

Clive Crook

In the following viewpoint, Clive Crook argues that a value-added tax, or VAT, is needed to pay for government spending. Crook claims that criticism of the VAT is misguided without another viable option. He claims that given the alternatives of severe spending cuts or drastic increases in income tax, the VAT is the best option to avoid a fiscal crisis. Crook is a senior editor of The Atlantic, *a columnist for* National Journal, *and a commentator for the* Financial Times.

As you read, consider the following questions:

1. According to Crook, what will neither Democrats nor Republicans discuss?

2. According to the author, to raise 5 percent of the gross domestic product (GDP) through a VAT, the tax rate would need to be what percentage?

Clive Crook, "Make a VAT Part of the Solution," *National Journal*, April 24, 2010. www.nationaljournal.com. Reproduced by permission.

3. Crook says that an alternative to the VAT is to cut federal spending by what percentage of the gross national product?

As an advocate of a value-added tax [VAT], I am pleased the idea is receiving wide discussion at last. In recent columns, George Will and Robert Samuelson poured scorn on the notion—but that is all right. It is better for a proposal to be attacked than ignored. If opposition to a VAT is stirring, I see this as a good sign.

Critics of a VAT

I admire both Will and Samuelson. I do not always agree with them—least of all with Will, because I am a wavering centrist rather than an outright conservative. But they always have interesting things to say, and VAT fans should take their arguments seriously.

Samuelson says: "Almost every pro-VAT argument is exaggerated, misleading, incomplete, or wrong. The VAT is being merchandised as an almost painless way to avoid deep spending cuts. The implicit, though often unstated, message is that a VAT could raise so much money, it could eliminate future deficits by itself. This reasoning, if embraced, would create staggering tax burdens and exempt us from a debate we desperately need ... How big a government do we want—and what can we afford?"

Will takes a more fundamentalist line. "When liberals advocate a VAT, conservatives should respond: Taxing consumption has merits, so we will consider it—after the 16th Amendment is repealed." He might go along with a VAT that replaces the income tax, but he objects to one that adds to it. He accuses the [President Barack] Obama administration of deliberately creating a fiscal crisis so that "the public can be panicked into accepting the addition of a VAT to the existing menu of taxes."

Both are right, of course, that the country cannot have everything it wants and needs to make choices. Neither Democrats nor Republicans want to discuss them. Democrats concentrate on the extra spending they see as desirable or necessary, and will work out how to pay for it later. Republicans are even further away from addressing the issue. They oppose any and all tax increases, yet swear to defend the most-expensive spending programs: Medicare, Social Security, and defense.

The Need to Pay for Spending

The question is how to bring the spending the country desires into line with the taxes it is willing to pay. Neither party even wants to think about it.

But when Samuelson says that the VAT proposal "exempts" the country from this overdue discussion, he loses me. Just the opposite—it puts the question of affordability on the table. The needed debate becomes impossible to avoid. He also says that VAT fans divert attention from affordability by presenting the tax as painless. Nonsense. Who among them is arguing that a VAT would be painless? It is self-evidently painful. That is the point. Moreover, it hurts everybody, unlike an income-tax hike confined to the "rich." If an advancing VAT does not get the country thinking about what it can afford, nothing will.

Samuelson is right about the underlying fiscal pressures. The aging of the population, together with relentlessly rising expectations, are going to force the costs of Social Security and Medicare much higher. On top of that, the country has just passed a health care reform law that—Congressional Budget Office estimates notwithstanding—is likely to raise long-term spending beyond revenues. The other huge spending category is defense, but there are no big, easy cuts there either. The world is still dangerous.

Federal spending is on course to be 25 percent of the economy in 2020, even after an extended economic recovery. That is up from 20 percent, on average, between 1970 and 2009. State spending has trended higher, too—a pattern that is unlikely to change. (The health care reform imposes a heavy burden of extra Medicaid spending on states.) Overall public spending is getting up toward European levels. But taxes have not gone up alongside, and the result is a long-term fiscal deficit of about 6 percent of gross domestic product. It cannot last. Something has to give.

The Drawbacks of a VAT

Obviously, the VAT has drawbacks—aside from the fact that it is a tax.

Its purported simplicity, as Samuelson notes, is partly an illusion. In practice, the VAT is not a uniform tax on consumption, as its advocates sometimes claim. Europe's governments grant exemptions or preferential rates to many categories of spending—food, children's clothes, rent, what have you.

Complexity aside, these exclusions narrow the tax base and mean that rates must be higher for any given amount of revenue collected. Raising 5 percent of GDP [gross domestic product] through a VAT would require a tax rate of well over 10 percent. A further complication in the U.S. is that states rely on sales taxes. They will resist the federal government's moving in on their preferred tax base. Getting around those complaints might lead to other complications.

But what tax is perfect? The question is, what are the relevant alternatives? Without comprehensive reform, the federal income tax is incapable of delivering the needed revenues. The fiscal gap is equivalent to well over half its total take.

The Tax Policy Center, under the joint sponsorship of the Urban Institute and the Brookings Institution, has calculated that a tax increase of nearly 40 percent would be needed to reduce—"not eliminate, just reduce," the center emphasizes—the deficit to 3 percent of GDP by 2015. The lowest income-tax rate would have to rise from 10 percent to 14 percent, and the top rate from 35 percent to 48 percent. If the increases were confined to households making more than $250,000, the top rate would need to double, to nearly 80 percent. "Such dramatic tax increases are politically untenable," the center says, "and still wouldn't come close to eliminating the deficit."

The Right Solution

If nothing else, these numbers underline the scale of the problem. The right solution is to do a lot of things, not just one. First and foremost, as Samuelson advises, look for spending cuts. Raise the retirement age. Pare back wasteful subsidies. Follow through on the cost-control mechanisms that the health care law introduced too tentatively. Look hard for savings in defense.

Then, however, combine these savings with higher revenues, again from different sources. A simpler income tax would help. Capping the deduction for employer-provided health insurance would raise revenue and strengthen the incentive for cost control in health care at the same time. Bring in a moderate carbon tax. And introduce a VAT—which, though imperfect, would do less economic harm than an equivalent rise in income taxes. To combine what is necessary with what is politically feasible can best be done by using all of the above.

[George] Will ends a recent column on the subject with this: "Because the 16th Amendment will not be repealed, adoption of a VAT would proclaim the impossibility of serious spending reductions, and hence would be the obituary for the Founders' vision of limited government." Well, for good or ill, that obituary was written decades ago. The Founders' vision of limited government died with the creation of Social Security and Medicare, if not before. The United States has built its welfare state, and now has to pay for it.

Samuelson agrees with Will that spending cuts should be the focus of attention, and that "simplistic VAT advocacy" shifts the focus elsewhere. "VAT enthusiasts need to answer two questions: What government spending would you cut? And how high would your VAT rates go?"

Fair questions, and I agree with the sentiment: Eternal vigilance on spending is necessary to check the relentless growth of government.

Cut Spending or Increase Taxes

But opponents of a VAT are surely under an even stronger obligation to say what spending they would cut, unless they are saying that a deficit of 6 percent of GDP is no problem. Let's hear from them. Show us how to cut 6 percent of GDP from federal spending—approximately a quarter of the current total—without popular outrage and real economic distress. Show us how to do it without gutting Social Security and Medicare, or seriously compromising national security. And tell us how to make it politically feasible.

I'll concede this much to Samuelson and Will: The superior efficiency of a VAT is a mixed blessing. Increasing a VAT, once you have it, is less damaging to the economy than raising the same amount of revenue from an unreformed income tax. So one result of a VAT might be less political resistance to higher taxes and bigger government.

Europe's experience seems to support this view. If blocking the growth of the state is your overriding priority, you might oppose a VAT precisely because, as taxes go, it is a good one. By the same logic, of course, you should strive to make the income tax even worse. The rule would be, collect revenue in the most damaging ways possible. That will raise the price of Big Government and tie the liberals' hands.

An interesting theory. While we debate it, the deficit sits there. Big Government is no longer a prospect to ward off. That choice has been made. One might regret it—but not as much as the consequences of refusing to pay for it.

| "The VAT—on top of all the other taxes Washington imposes—is a terrible idea."

A Value-Added Tax Would Be Bad for America

Daniel J. Mitchell

In the following viewpoint, Daniel J. Mitchell argues that impos-ing a value-added tax, or VAT, on top of all the other taxes Americans currently pay is a bad idea. Mitchell claims that the government wants the VAT so it can increase spending, which he opposes. He points to statistics from European countries to sup-port his view that the VAT is linked with a higher overall tax burden and increased government spending. Mitchell is a senior fellow at the Cato Institute, specializing in tax reform and supply-side tax policy. He is co-author, with Chris Edwards, of Global Tax Revolution: The Rise of Tax Competition and the Battle to Defend It.

As you read, consider the following questions:

1. According to Mitchell, what are two virtues of the value-added tax?

Daniel J. Mitchell, "VAT Attack: Beware: 'Value-Added Tax' Is an Economy-Killer," *New York Post*, April 8, 2010. www.nypost.com. Reproduced by permission.

2. Annual federal spending rose by what amount from 2001 to the last budget of President George W. Bush, according to the author?

3. Mitchell claims that in 2006, the average tax burden was how much higher in advanced European economies, the EU (European Union)-15 nations, compared with the United States?

One of President [Barack] Obama's top economic advisers, former Fed [Federal Reserve] chief Paul Volcker, suggested this week that it's time for America to adopt a VAT, or value-added tax. The White House yesterday [April 7, 2010] downplayed the idea—but it's sure to resurface: It's an inevitable consequence of a government that's too big now and likely to grow even bigger thanks to Washington's reckless spending spree.

Value-Added Tax

Don't get me wrong: The VAT—on top of all the other taxes Washington imposes—is a terrible idea. Imposing it would pretty well finish the transformation of our country into a European-style slow-growth nation. The right way to close Uncle Sam's gaping deficits is to reverse the continued explosion of federal spending.

The VAT is a type of national sales tax, levied on the value-added at each stage of production. Consider a piece of furniture: The VAT would be imposed when the raw timber is sold, when the sawmill produces lumber, when the manufacturer builds a chair, a tax at the wholesaler level and then when a retailer sells the chair to a consumer.

To avoid double taxation, each seller along the way gets a credit for taxes paid at earlier stages of the production process. So the final tax to the consumer, at least in theory, is the same as a retail sales tax of the same amount.

The VAT has its virtues: As a single-rate, consumption-based system, much like the flat tax or national sales tax, it would introduce far fewer economic distortions than today's income tax—and a heckuva lot less paperwork.

That would be a persuasive argument—*if* proponents wanted a VAT to replace the Internal Revenue code. But that's not what's intended by Volcker—or Senate Budget Committee Chairman Kent Conrad and House Speaker Nancy Pelosi, who've also been chatting up the VAT.

The Size of Government

The politicians want a VAT, and they want to keep the income tax. (To be more accurate, they want a VAT and to *raise* other taxes as well.)

They want the cash, of course, so they can continue buying votes by spending other people's money.

This decade already has seen a huge expansion of government. In the [President George W.] Bush years, federal spending rose from $1.8 trillion in 2001 to $3.5 trillion in the last Bush budget. Now President Obama is well on the way to doubling outlays yet again.

He has already saddled the economy with $800 billion of "stimulus" and a giant new health-care entitlement, and his proposals for next year will push the federal budget even higher.

Meanwhile, our aging population and the built-in growth in federal programs like Medicare, Medicaid and Social Security has a dramatic expansion in the size of government set to occur automatically in coming decades.

Simply stated, there's no way to finance all this new spending *without* an added broad-based tax. But this is exactly why we should vigorously resist a VAT.

Blocking a VAT may not be sufficient to control the size of government, but it's necessary. Handing Washington a whole new source of revenue would be akin to giving keys to a liquor store to a bunch of alcoholics.

The Overall Tax Burden

The real-world evidence shows that VATs are strongly linked with both higher overall tax burdens and more government spending. In 1965, before the VAT swept across Europe, the average tax burden for advanced European [Union] economies (the EU-15) was 27.7 percent of economic output, versus 24.7 percent of GDP [gross domestic product] in the United States.

But the Europeans began imposing VATs in the late 1960s, and now the European Union requires all members to have a VAT of at least 15 percent. Good news has not followed. By 2006, the average tax burden for EU-15 nations had climbed to 39.8 percent, versus 28 percent in the United States.

The spending side? In 1965, pre-VAT, government spending in EU-15 nations averaged 30.1 percent of GDP, against 28.3 percent in the United States. By 2007, government spending consumed 47.1 percent of GDP in EU-15, significantly higher than the US burden of 35.3 percent.

Nor has the VAT stopped Europe from raising other taxes.

Taxes on income and profits consumed 8.8 percent of GDP in Europe in 1965—*below* the US level of 11.9 percent. By 2006, the European burden had climbed to 13.8 percent of GDP, slightly higher than the 13.5 percent US figure. (The same trend holds for corporate-tax data.)

Today's income-tax system is a nightmarish combination of class warfare and corrupt loopholes. But adding a VAT solves none of those problems, it merely gives politicians more money to spend and a chance to auction off a new set of tax breaks to interest groups. That's good for Washington, but bad for America.

▌ *"The estate tax needs to go."*

The Estate Tax Should Be Repealed Permanently

Arthur B. Laffer

In the following viewpoint, Arthur B. Laffer argues that the estate tax should be eliminated. He contends that taxing the wealthy at death does little to redistribute wealth and irrationally encourages the wealthy to spend all their money before they die. He claims that money is wasted in compliance fees and in avoiding the tax, and that the tax needs to be permanently repealed. Laffer is the founder and chairman of Laffer Associates, an economic research and consulting firm, and a former member of President Ronald Reagan's Economic Policy Advisory Board.

As you read, consider the following questions:

1. According to Laffer, President Barack Obama has proposed prolonging the estate tax with a top tax rate of what amount?

2. The author claims that the total monies collected each year from the estate tax amount to what percentage of federal tax receipts?

Arthur B. Laffer, "Spend It in Vegas or Die Paying Taxes," *Wall Street Journal*, April 2, 2009, p. A19. Reproduced by permission.

3. What percentage of Americans do not have to pay the estate tax, according to the author?

In most cases, people who inherit wealth are lucky by an accident of birth and really don't "deserve" their inheritance any more than people who don't inherit wealth. After all, few of us get to choose our parents. It's also arguable that inherited wealth sometimes induces slothfulness and overindulgence. But the facts that beneficiaries of inheritances are just lucky and that the actual inheritance may make beneficiaries less productive don't justify having an estate tax.

The Distribution of Wealth

These same observations about serendipitous birth can be made for intelligence, education, attractiveness, health, size, gender, disposition, race, etc. And yet no one would suggest that the government should remove any portion of these attributes from people simply because they came from their parents. Surely we have not moved into Kurt Vonnegut's world of Harrison Bergeron [from his science fiction short story of the same name].

President Barack Obama has proposed prolonging the federal estate tax rather than ending it in 2010, as is scheduled under current law. The president's plan would extend this year's $3.5 million exemption level and the 45% top rate. But will this really help America recover from recession and reduce our growing deficits? In order to assess the pros and cons of the estate tax, we should focus on its impact on those who bequeath wealth, not on those who receive wealth.

Advocates of the estate tax argue that such a tax will reduce the concentrations of wealth in a few families, but there is little evidence to suggest that the estate tax has much, if any, impact on the distribution of wealth. To see the silliness of using the estate tax as a tool to redistribute wealth, realize that those who die and leave estates would be taxed just as much if they bequeathed their money to poor people as they would if they left their money to rich people. If the objective were to redistribute, surely, an inheritance tax (a tax on the recipients) would make far more sense than an estate tax.

Indeed, from a societal standpoint, inheritance is an unmitigated good. Passing on to successive generations greater health, wealth and wisdom is what society in general, and America specifically, is all about. Imagine what America would look like today if our forefathers had been selfish and had left us nothing. We have all benefited greatly from a history of intergenerational American generosity. But just being an American is as much an accident of birth as being the child of wealthy parents. If you are an American, it's likely because ancestors of yours chose to become Americans and also chose to have children.

A Senseless Tax

In its most basic form, it's about as silly an idea as can be imagined that America in the aggregate can increase the standards of living of future generations by taxing individual Americans for passing on higher standards of living to future generations of Americans of their choice. Clearly, taxing estates at death will induce people who wish to leave estates to future generations to leave smaller estates and to find ways to avoid estate taxes. On a conceptual level, it makes no sense to tax estates at death.

Study after study finds that the estate tax significantly reduces the size of estates and, as an added consequence, reduces the nation's capital stock and income. This common sense finding is documented ad nauseam in the 2006 U.S. Joint Economic Committee Report on the Costs and Consequences of the Federal Estate Tax. The Joint Economic Committee estimates that the estate tax has reduced the capital stock by approximately $850 billion because it reduces incen-

The Impact of the Estate Tax

To understand why steep marginal rates like the death tax distort economic activity, it is important to consider a cornerstone of economic analysis: the fact that people make decisions on the margin. As a practical example, imagine an entrepreneur who is worth just under $3.5 million with a growing business. He wishes to pass this business on to his son or daughter, but after his total worth exceeds $3.5 million dollars, any additional wealth he creates is subject to a steep 45% tax rate at death. Before crossing the margin into estate tax territory, many entrepreneurs choose to cut back on further expansion of their businesses. When businessmen know that the death tax will cut any future accumulation in half, they are much less likely to grow their business above the exemption amount. For many, this exemption amount becomes a ceiling above which the now-measly profits are not worth the extra effort. Such a tax policy discourages small business expansion, and thus also discourages job creation. This is why steep marginal tax rates, like the death tax, are so economically harmful.

Palmer Schoening and Patrick Fagan,
"Repealing Death Tax Will Create Jobs and Boost Economy,"
Insight, September 2009. www.frc.org.

tives to save and invest, has excessively high compliance costs, and results in significant economic inefficiencies.

Today in America you can take your after-tax income and go to Las Vegas and carouse, gamble, drink and smoke, and as far as our government is concerned that's just fine. But if you take that same after-tax income and leave it to your children and grandchildren, the government will tax that after-tax income one additional time at rates up to 55%. I especially like an oft-quoted line from Joseph Stiglitz and David L. Bevan, who wrote in the *Greek Economic Review*, "Of course, prohibitively high inheritance tax rates generate no revenue; they simply force the individual to consume his income during his lifetime." Hurray for Vegas.

The High Cost of Compliance and Avoidance

If you're rich enough, however, you can hire professionals who can, for a price, show you how to avoid estate taxes. Many of the very largest estates are so tax-sheltered that the inheritances go to their beneficiaries having paid little or no taxes at all. And all the costs associated with these tax shelters and tax avoidance schemes are pure wastes for the country as a whole and exist solely to circumvent the estate tax. The estate tax in and of itself causes people to waste resources.

Again, a number of studies suggest that the costs of sheltering estates from the tax man actually are about as high as the total tax revenues collected from the estate tax. And these estimates don't even take into account lost output, employment and production resulting from perverse incentives. This makes the estate tax one of the least efficient taxes. And yet for all the hardship and expense associated with the estate tax, the total monies collected in any one year account for only about 1% of federal tax receipts.

It is important to realize that less than half of the estates that must go through the burden of complying with the paperwork and reporting requirements of the tax actually pay even a nickel of the tax. And the largest estates that actually do pay taxes generally pay lower marginal tax rates than smaller estates because of tax shelters. The inmates really are running the asylum.

Eliminate the Estate Tax

In 1982, Californians overwhelmingly voted to eliminate the state's estate tax. It seems that even in the highest taxed state in the nation there are some taxes voters cannot abide. It shouldn't surprise anyone that ultra-wealthy liberal Sen. Howard Metzenbaum, supporter of the estate tax and lifetime resident of Ohio, where there is a state estate tax, chose to die as a resident of Florida, where there is no state estate tax. Differential state estate-tax rates incentivize people to move from state to state. Global estate tax rates do the same thing, only the moves are from country to country. In 2005 the U.S., at a 47% marginal tax rate, had the third highest estate tax rate of the 50 countries covered in a 2005 report by Price Waterhouse Coopers, LLP. A full 26 countries had no "Inheritance/Death" tax rate at all.

In the summary of its 2006 report, the Joint Economic Committee wrote, "The detrimental effects of the estate tax are grossly disproportionate to the modest amount of federal revenues it raises (if it raises any net revenue at all)." Even economists in favor of the estate tax concede that its current structure does not work. Henry Aaron and Alicia Munnell concluded, "In short, the estate and gift taxes in the United States have failed to achieve their intended purposes. They raise little revenue. They impose large excess burdens. They are unfair."

For all of these reasons, the estate tax needs to go, along with the step-up basis at death of capital gains (which values an asset not at the purchase price but at the price at the buyer's death). On purely a static basis, the Joint Tax Committee estimates that over the period 2011 through 2015, the static revenue losses from eliminating the estate tax would be $281 billion, while the additional capital gains tax receipts from repeal of the step-up basis would be $293 billion.

To counter the fact that economists such as I obsess about the deleterious effects of the estate tax, advocates of the estate tax note with some pride that 98% of Americans will never pay this tax. Let's make it 100%, and I'll get off my soapbox.

| "Congress must permanently reinstate
| the estate tax for 2010 and subsequent
| years."

The Estate Tax Should Not Be Repealed

Americans for a Fair Estate Tax

In the following viewpoint, Americans for a Fair Estate Tax (AFET) argue that the estate tax needs to be retained. AFET contends that the revenue from the estate tax is needed and that it is fair and justified that wealthy Americans not be allowed to pass on tax-free inheritance money. AFET recommends that the exemption be lowered, the tax rate be raised, and the tax be simplified. AFET is a coalition of national and state organizations working to retain the federal estate tax.

As you read, consider the following questions:

1. Americans for a Fair Estate Tax claim that the cost of a full repeal of the estate tax over ten years is what?

2. According to the author, how many small business and small farm estates paid any estate tax in 2009?

3. How many states currently have estate taxes, according to Americans for a Fair Estate Tax?

Americans for a Fair Estate Tax, "Statement of Principles on Estate Tax Legislation," 2010. Reproduced by permission.

Our nation desperately needs revenue to invest in education, health, nutrition, and other priorities to promote a competitive workforce and ensure opportunity for every American. Only one-third of working adults have a college degree. One out of three Americans lacked health insurance at least once over the last couple years. Poverty, joblessness, and home foreclosures are harsh realities for millions of Americans.

The Elimination of the Estate Tax

We are told over and over again that increased investments in the American people are not affordable because the federal budget deficit is too great. And yet, Congress has gradually eliminated an important revenue source that can help fund these priorities and reduce the budget deficit.

Through a period of war, natural disaster, and now the worst economic downturn since the Great Depression, the [President George W.] Bush Administration and Congress set in place the gradual elimination of the federal estate tax. Since 2001, the tax was cut to exempt more and more estates so that in 2009, only one-quarter of one percent of all estates in the U.S. were expected to pay the tax. In 2009, only individuals with estates worth more than $3.5 million ($7 million for married couples) were subject to the tax. In January 2010, the estate tax was completely eliminated for one year.

The Purposes of the Estate Tax

The federal estate tax has been repealed for 2010 and under current law will reappear in 2011. Congress must permanently reinstate the estate tax for 2010 and subsequent years because it serves these crucial purposes:

• *The estate tax raises revenue that we need to invest in the American people.* When Congress enacted the gradual repeal of the estate tax in 2001, it did not want to own up to the enormous cost of full repeal, which would exceed *$800 billion* over ten years. Therefore, after a year of outright repeal in 2010, the legislation calls for the estate tax to return to its old levels starting in 2011. Supporters of the Bush estate tax repeal assumed in 2001 that Congress would not allow the tax to be reinstated. Now that repeal has taken effect, Congress must take a hard look at the damage it is inflicting. Continuing the repeal will deepen the budget deficit by about $800 billion between 2012 and 2021. Keeping the estate tax at its 2009 level will cost about $400 billion over ten years.

• *The estate tax ensures that families who have benefited the most from public goods pay their fair share to maintain them.* Families that have accumulated massive fortunes in America could not have done so without the infrastructure, educated workforce, stability and other public benefits that taxes make possible. Society only works when *everyone* contributes to the common good.

• *The federal estate tax provides a check on the concentration of power in the hands of those born into great wealth.* Such a concentration of power is contrary to American values and democratic principles. This is a growing problem today, as hard-working Americans are finding fewer opportunities for success because education and other paths to advancement are increasingly out of reach. The United States now has the greatest concentration of wealth in the hands of the rich in nearly a century. As billionaire Warren Buffet reminds us, "Without the estate tax, you in effect will have an aristocracy of wealth, which means you pass down the ability to command the resources of the nation based on heredity rather than merit."

• *The estate tax corrects a feature of our tax system that would otherwise allow certain income to escape taxation entirely.* Over half the value of inherited estates is capital gains income that has *never* been taxed. Most large estates include assets such as real estate, stocks or bonds. Any increase in the value of these assets is capital gain income that would be subject to the income tax if they were sold during the owner's lifetime. However, this income is not subject to the income tax if the owner dies and leaves it to an heir.

• *The estate tax encourages charitable giving.* The estate tax is not imposed on assets bequeathed to charity. Many wealthy individuals take advantage of this unlimited deduction for charitable giving. In 2004, the Congressional Budget Office estimated that if the estate tax had not existed in 2000, charitable donations would have been $13–$25 billion lower that year.

Who Pays the Estate Tax

Despite claims to the contrary, the estate tax does NOT affect the vast majority of small businesses and family farms. The Brookings/Urban Institute Tax Policy Center estimates that in 2009, only eighty small business and small farm estates *nationwide* owed *any* estate tax, and these estates paid an average tax of only 14 percent. This has not stopped estate tax opponents from spending millions in lobbying and advertising claiming that the estate tax hurts small businesses and family farms. This is simply a ruse to convince average Americans to support another massive tax cut for the wealthy that they would otherwise reject.

We call on Congress and the President to take the following steps when addressing the estate tax:

1. *Exempt no more than the first $2 million ($4 million for married couples) of assets in an estate.*

A $2 million per-spouse exemption for the estate tax was in effect from 2006 through 2008. This shielded over 99 percent of the estates of people who died during those years from taxation. A $2 million per-spouse exemption is also twice as large as the exemption that takes effect in 2011 under current law.

2. *Set a tax rate of no less than 45 percent for the taxable portion of estates, with an additional 10 percent tax on the taxable portion exceeding $10 million.*

The taxable portion of an estate includes assets in excess of the exemption, and it excludes any assets bequeathed to a spouse or charity. Therefore, even if the taxable portion of an estate is taxed at a statutory rate of 45 percent, the *effective* tax rate on the entire estate, i.e. how much is actually paid, is much lower.

A fundamental tenet of a fair tax system is that those who have the greatest ability to pay should pay a larger share. Great wealth is the best indicator of ability to pay. The estate tax should continue to target the very wealthy, and the largest estates should be taxed at a higher rate.

The Need for Changes to the Tax

3. Restore a credit for estate and inheritance taxes.

The credit for state estate and inheritance taxes was gradually repealed under the tax cut legislation enacted in 2001, but will reappear in 2011. This credit allows states to share in estate tax revenues without having to administer a separate state tax.

Before the 2001 estate tax cuts were enacted, all 50 states had a tax on estates or inheritances. Many of these taxes have since disappeared because they were tied to the credit in the federal estate tax. Currently, only 20 states have such taxes. This is particularly problematic now, as this loss of tax revenue contributes to the severe budget shortfalls that many states are facing.

4. Simplify the estate tax.

The estate tax should be simplified in two ways. First, the gift tax, estate tax, and generation-skipping transfer taxes should be "reunified," so that transfers made during the lifetime or at death are subject to the same rules, exemptions, and tax rates. This will ensure tax fairness and reduce the need, and incentive, for complicated tax planning.

Second, the estate tax should allow for the "portability" of any unused estate tax exemption from one spouse to another.

If one spouse dies without using his or her entire $2 million exemption, the unused portion should automatically transfer to the surviving spouse. This would greatly simplify estate tax planning for many Americans and avoid the need to split up and re-title assets or set up complicated trusts. It also would eliminate situations in which some families have to pay the estate tax just because they failed to plan for it.

Periodical Bibliography

The following articles have been selected to supplement the diverse views presented in this chapter.

Karlyn Bowman	"A Killer Tax," Forbes.com, December 7, 2009.
Gary Burtless	"Should There Be a VAT in America's Future?" *National Journal*, April 26, 2010.
Lee Farris	"Estate Tax Preserves Opportunity in U.S.," *Oneida Daily Dispatch* (Oneida, NY), December 15, 2009.
Chye-Ching Huang	"The High Cost of Estate Tax Repeal," Center on Budget and Policy Priorities, January 28, 2009.
Elizabeth McNichol	"Stalled Estate Tax Proposal Could Threaten State Revenues That Support Education, Public Safety, and Other Key Services," Center on Budget and Policy Priorities, May 20, 2010.
Daniel J. Mitchell	"'Death Tax' Destroys Wealth," *USA Today*, October 1, 2009.
Terry Neese and Bethany Lowe	"Estate Tax Myths," *Brief Analysis No. 678*, National Center for Policy Analysis, October 1, 2009.
Robert J. Samuelson	"The VAT Isn't an Easy Fix for Budget Woes," *Washington Post*, April 19, 2010.
Palmer Shoening and Patrick Fagan	"Repealing Death Tax Will Create Jobs and Boost Economy," *Insight*, September 2009.
George F. Will	"The Perils of the Value-Added Tax," *Washington Post*, April 18, 2010.

OPPOSING
VIEWPOINTS®
SERIES

CHAPTER 4

How Should the US Tax System Be Reformed?

Chapter Preface

It would be challenging to find an American who believes the current US tax system needs no reform at all. But proposals for reform range from those calling for incremental change to the existing system, to those calling for a completely new model of taxation.

Among the proposals for incremental change are various calls to change the guidelines for the collection of federal income tax and state income tax. Tax policy experts John S. Irons and John Podesta, for example, argue that the progressive tax structure needs to be restored to insure that corporations and wealthy Americans are paying a higher effective tax rate than are low-income Americans. They argue that the tax cuts of 2001 and 2003, instituted under President George W. Bush, made the tax system less fair and unfairly burdened those with lower incomes. One of their proposals is to tax all forms of income at the same rate in an effort to "end preferential treatment for income from capital (wealth) over income from work by setting capital gains and dividend taxes equal to the tax rates on ordinary income."[1] However, Duncan Currie, deputy managing editor of *National Review*, disagrees with this call for incremental change, claiming that the US tax system "is already highly progressive." He claims, "America's top income earners now shoulder a greater share of the federal tax burden than they did when President [George W.] Bush first took office, and they shoulder a *much* greater share than they did in the early 1980s."[2]

People such as former Republican presidential candidate, Steve Forbes, have called for more sweeping reform. In his 2005 book, *Flat Tax Revolution: Using a Postcard to Abolish the*

---

1. John S. Irons and John Podesta, "A Tax Plan for Progressives," *American Prospect*, June 2005.
2. Duncan Currie, "America Has a Highly Progressive Tax System," *American*, October 24, 2008.

IRS, Forbes calls for a 17 percent flat tax for all individuals and an end to the Internal Revenue Service (IRS) and its extensive tax filing paperwork. Also advocating radical change is Yale Law School professor Michael J. Graetz. In his book, *100 Million Unnecessary Returns: A Simple, Fair, and Competitive Tax Plan for the United States*, Graetz argues for a value-added tax to replace federal income tax for most Americans. Both Forbes and Graetz cite simplicity as a virtue of their respective models, but not all are convinced of this virtue. Economist Robert Kuttner claims, "Most tax complexity is the problem—and the opportunity—of those in the upper brackets." Kuttner claims that making the system simpler should not be achieved by sweeping reform but by repealing "tax preferences that cause most of the system's complexity, regressivity, and failure to collect adequate revenues."[3]

Clearly, calls for reform of the US tax system abound. The big question is whether the US tax system needs tinkering or complete replacement.

3. Robert Kuttner, "The Simplification Dodge," *American Prospect Online*, March 24, 2008. www.prospect.org.

| "It's unfortunate that the United States is missing out on the tax reform revolution."

A Flat Tax Should Replace the Current System

Daniel J. Mitchell

In the following viewpoint, Daniel J. Mitchell argues that the United States should join the flat tax revolution. Mitchell claims that since the flat tax was seriously considered in the mid-1990s, there have been several promising examples of nations who have adopted a flat tax system around the world. He claims that the flat tax system would be beneficial for the United States. Mitchell is a senior fellow at the Cato Institute, specializing in tax reform and supply-side tax policy. He also is co-author, with Chris Edwards, of Global Tax Revolution: The Rise of Tax Competition and the Battle to Defend It.

As you read, consider the following questions:

1. According to Mitchell, under the flat tax proposed by Dick Armey, households would have to pay how much tax on wages, salaries, and pensions?

Daniel J. Mitchell, "The Global Flat Tax Revolution," *Cato Policy Report*, vol. 29, no. 4, July–August 2007, pp. 1, 10–12. Reproduced by permission.

2. What country, which adopted the flat tax in 1994, does the author use as an example of a nation that adopted a flat tax system successfully?

3. The author claims that the top income tax rate has dropped by how many percentage points since 1980?

In the early 1990s, Rep. Dick Armey (R-TX) proposed a flat tax. He would have junked the Internal Revenue Code and replaced it with a system designed to raise revenue in a much less destructive fashion. The core principles were to tax income at one low rate, to eliminate double taxation of saving and investment, and to wipe out the special preferences, credits, exemptions, deductions, and other loopholes that caused complexity, distortions, and corruption.

The Flat Tax Proposal

The flat tax never made it through Congress, but it's been adopted by more than a dozen other countries since 1994.

It's unfortunate that the United States is missing out on the tax reform revolution. Instead of the hundreds of forms demanded by the current tax system, the Armey flat tax would have required just two postcards. Households would have used the individual postcard to pay a 17 percent tax on wages, salary, and pensions, though a generous family-based allowance (more than $30,000 for a family of four) meant that there was no tax on the income needed to cover basic expenses.

Taxes on other types of income would have been calculated using the second postcard, which would have been filed by every business regardless of its size or structure. Simply stated, there would have been a 17 percent tax on net income, which would have been calculated by subtracting wages, input costs, and investment expenditures from total receipts.

While the simplicity and low tax rate were obvious selling points, the flat tax also eliminated various forms of double taxation, ending the bias against income that was saved and invested. In other words, the IRS [Internal Revenue Service] got to tax income only one time. The double tax on dividends would have been completely eliminated. The death tax also was to be wiped out, as was the capital gains tax, and all saving would have received "Roth IRA" [individual retirement account] treatment.

Another key feature of the flat tax was the repeal of special tax breaks. With the exception of a family-based allowance, there would have been no tax preferences. Lawmakers no longer would have been able to swap loopholes for campaign cash. It also would have encouraged businesses to focus on creating value for shareholders and consumers instead of trying to manipulate the tax code. Last but not least, the flat tax would have created a "territorial" system, meaning that the IRS no longer would have been charged with taxing Americans on income earned—and subject to tax—in other jurisdictions.

A Failed Attempt at Reform

Proponents correctly argued that a flat tax would improve America's economic performance and boost competitiveness. And after Republicans first took control of Congress [in 1995], it appeared that tax reform was possible. At one point, the debate was about, not whether there should be tax reform, but whether the Internal Revenue Code should be replaced by a flat tax or a national sales tax (which shared the flat tax's key principles of taxing economic activity only one time and at one low rate).

Notwithstanding this momentum in the mid-1990s, there ultimately was no serious legislative effort to reform the tax system. In part, that was because of White House opposition. The [Bill] Clinton administration rejected reform, largely relying on class-warfare arguments that a flat tax would benefit the so-called rich. But President Clinton wasn't the only obstacle. Congressional Democrats were almost universally hostile to tax reform, and a significant number of Republicans were reluctant to support a proposal that was opposed by well-connected interest groups.

The Flat Tax Around the World

One of the stumbling blocks to tax reform was the absence of "real-world" examples. When Armey first proposed his flat tax, the only recognized jurisdiction with a flat tax was Hong Kong. And even though Hong Kong enjoyed rapid economic growth, lawmakers seemed to think that the then-British colony was a special case and that it would be inappropriate to draw any conclusions from it about the desirability of a flat tax in the United States.

Today, much of the world seems to have learned the lessons that members of Congress didn't. Beginning with Estonia in 1994, a growing number of nations have joined the flat tax club. There are now 17 jurisdictions that have some form of flat tax, and two more nations are about to join the club. . . . Most of the new flat tax nations are former Soviet republics or former Soviet bloc nations, perhaps because people who suffered under communism are less susceptible to class-warfare rhetoric about "taxing the rich."

Flat Tax Lessons

The flat tax revolution raises three important questions: Why is it happening? What does the future hold? Should American policymakers learn any lessons?

The answer to the first question is a combination of principled leadership, tax competition, and learning by example. Flat tax pioneers such as Mart Laar (prime minister of Estonia), Andrei Illarionov (chief economic adviser to the president in Russia), and Ivan Miklos (finance minister in Slovakia) were motivated at least in part by their understanding of good tax policy and their desire to implement pro-growth reforms. But tax competition also has been an important factor, particularly in the recent wave of flat tax reforms. In a global economy, lawmakers increasingly realize that it is important to lower tax rates and reduce discriminatory burdens on saving and investment. A better fiscal climate plays a key role both in luring jobs and capital from other nations and in reducing the incentive for domestic taxpayers to shift economic activity to other nations.

Moreover, politicians are influenced by real-world evidence. Nations that have adopted flat tax systems generally have experienced very positive outcomes. Economic growth increases, unemployment drops, and tax compliance improves. Nations such as Estonia and Slovakia are widely viewed as role models since both have engaged in dramatic reform and are reaping enormous economic benefits. Policymakers in other nations see those results and conclude that tax reform is a relatively risk-free proposition. That is especially important since international bureaucracies such as the International Monetary Fund [IMF] usually try to discourage governments from lowering tax rates and adopting pro-growth reforms.

Countries with Flat Tax Systems

The answer to the second question is that more nations will probably join the flat tax club. Three nations currently are pursuing tax reform. Albania is on the verge of adopting a low-rate flat tax [adopted in 2009], as is East Timor [adopted in 2008] (though the IMF predictably is pushing for a needlessly high tax rate). A 15 percent flat tax has been proposed in the Czech Republic [adopted in 2008], though the political outlook is unclear because the government does not have an absolute majority in parliament.

It is also worth noting that countries with flat taxes are now competing to lower their tax rates. Estonia's rate already is down from 26 percent to 22 percent, and it will drop to 18 percent by 2011. The new prime minister's party, meanwhile, wants the rate eventually to settle at 12 percent. Lithuania's

Flat Tax Prosperity

Because the flat tax treats all economic activity equally, it will promote greater economic efficiency and increased prosperity. When saving is no longer taxed twice, people will save and invest more, leading to higher productivity and greater take-home pay. When marginal tax rates are lower, people will work more, start more businesses, and devote fewer resources to tax avoidance and evasion. And because tax rules will be uniform, people will base their financial decisions on common-sense economics, not arcane tax law.

Testimony of Richard K. Armey, Chairman, Freedom Works,
before the Senate Committee on Appropriations,
Subcommittee on the District of Columbia, March 8, 2006.

flat rate also has been reduced, falling from 33 percent to 27 percent, and is scheduled to fall to 24 percent next year [2008]. Macedonia's rate is scheduled to drop to 10 percent next year, and Montenegro's flat tax rate will fall to 9 percent in 2010—giving it the lowest flat tax rate in the world (though one could argue that places like the Cayman Islands and the Bahamas have flat taxes with rates of zero).

The continuing shift to flat tax systems and lower rates is rather amusing since an IMF study from last year claimed: "Looking forward, the question is not so much whether more countries will adopt a flat tax as whether those that have will move away from it." In reality, there is every reason to think that more nations will adopt flat tax systems and that tax competition will play a key role in pushing tax rates even lower.

The Flat Tax in America

For American taxpayers, the key question is whether politicians in Washington are paying attention to the global flat tax revolution and learning the appropriate lessons. There is no clear answer to this question. Policymakers certainly are aware that the flat tax is spreading around the world. Mart Laar, Andrei Illarionov, Ivan Miklos, and other international reformers have spoken several times to American audiences. President [George W.] Bush has specifically praised the tax reforms in Estonia, Russia, and Slovakia. And groups like the Cato Institute are engaged in ongoing efforts to educate policymakers about the positive benefits of global tax reform.

But it is important also to be realistic about the lessons that can be learned. The United States already is a wealthy economy, so it is very unlikely that a flat tax would generate the stupendous annual growth rates enjoyed by nations such as Estonia and Slovakia. The United States also has a very high rate of tax compliance, so it would be unwise to expect a huge "Laffer Curve" effect of additional tax revenue similar to what nations like Russia experienced.

It is also important to explain to policymakers that not all flat tax systems are created equal. Indeed, none of the world's flat tax systems is completely consistent with the pure model proposed by Professors Robert Hall and Alvin Rabushka in their book, *The Flat Tax*. Nations such as Russia and Lithuania, for instance, have substantial differences between the tax rates on personal and corporate income (even Hong Kong has a small gap). Serbia's flat tax applies only to labor income, making it a very tenuous member of the flat tax club. Although information for some nations is incomplete, it appears that all flat tax nations have at least some double taxation of income that is saved and invested (though Estonia, Slovakia, and Hong Kong get pretty close to an ideal system). Moreover, it does not appear that any nation other than Estonia permits immediate expensing of business investment expenditures.

(The corporate income tax in Estonia has been abolished, for all intents and purposes, since businesses only have to pay withholding tax on dividend payments.)

Policymakers also should realize that a flat tax is not a silver bullet capable of solving all of a nation's problems. From a fiscal policy perspective, for instance, the Russian flat tax has been successful. But Russia still has many problems, including a lack of secure property rights and excessive government intervention. Iraq is another example. The U.S. government imposed a flat tax there in 2004, but even the best tax code is unlikely to have much effect in a nation suffering from instability and violence.

The Flat Tax Revolution

With all these caveats, the flat tax revolution nonetheless has bolstered the case for better tax policy, both in America and elsewhere in the world. In particular, there is now more support for lower rates instead of higher rates because of evidence that marginal tax rates have an impact on productive behavior and tax compliance. Among developed nations, the top personal income tax rate is 25 percentage points lower today than it was in 1980. Similarly, the average corporate tax rate in developed nations has dropped by 20 percentage points during the same period. Those reforms are not consequences of the flat tax revolution. [British Prime Minister] Margaret Thatcher and Ronald Reagan started the move toward less punitive tax rates more than 25 years ago. But the flat tax revolution has helped cement those gains and is encouraging additional rate reductions.

Moreover, there is now increased appreciation for reducing the tax bias against income that is saved and invested. Indeed, Sweden and Australia have abolished death taxes, and Denmark and the Netherlands have eliminated wealth taxes. Other nations are lowering taxes on capital income, much as the United States has reduced the double taxation of dividends and capital gains to 15 percent. And although the United States is a clear laggard in the move toward simpler and more neutral tax regimes, the flat tax revolution is helping to teach lawmakers about the benefits of a system that does not penalize or subsidize various behaviors.

The flat tax revolution also suggests that the politics of class warfare is waning. For much of the 20th century, policymakers subscribed to the notion that the tax code should be used to penalize those who contribute most to economic growth. Raising revenue was also a factor, to be sure, but many politicians seem to have been more motivated by the ideological impulse that rich people should be penalized with higher tax rates. If nothing else, the growing community of flat tax nations shows that class-warfare objections can be overcome.

Obstacles to Tax Reform

Although the flat tax revolution has been impressive, there are still significant hurdles. Most important, international bureaucracies are obstacles to tax reform, both because they are ideologically opposed to the flat tax and because they represent the interests of high-tax nations that want tax harmonization rather than tax competition. The Organization for Economic Cooperation and Development [OECD], for instance, has a "harmful tax competition" project that seeks to hinder the flow of labor and capital from high-tax nations to low-tax jurisdictions. The OECD even produced a 1998 report stating that tax competition "may hamper the application of progressive tax rates and the achievement of redistributive goals." In 2000 the Paris-based bureaucracy created a blacklist of low-tax jurisdictions, threatening them with financial protectionism if they did not change their domestic laws to discourage capital from nations with oppressive tax regimes.

The OECD has been strongly criticized for seeking to undermine fiscal sovereignty, but its efforts also should be seen as a direct attack on tax reform. Two of the key principles of the flat tax are eliminating double taxation and eliminating territorial taxation. These principles, however, are directly contrary to the OECD's anti-tax competition project—which is primarily focused on enabling high-tax nations to track (and tax) flight capital. That necessarily means that the OECD wants countries to double tax income that is saved and invested, and to impose that bad policy on an extraterritorial basis.

The OECD is not alone in the fight. The European Commission also has a number of anti-tax-competition schemes. The United Nations, too, is involved and even has a proposal for an International Tax Organization. All of those international bureaucracies are asserting the right to dictate "best practices" that would limit the types of tax policy a jurisdiction could adopt. Unfortunately, their definition of best practices is based on what makes life easier for politicians rather than what promotes prosperity.

Fortunately, these efforts to create a global tax cartel have largely been thwarted, and an "OPEC [organization of the Petroleum Exporting Countries] for politicians" is still just a gleam in the eyes of French and German politicians. That means that tax competition is still flourishing, and that means that the flat tax club is likely to get larger rather than smaller.

| "A flat tax would discourage saving for retirement and providing health insurance."

A Flat Tax Should Not Replace the Current System

Holley Ulbrich

In the following viewpoint, Holley Ulbrich argues that the proposal to implement a flat tax should be resisted. Ulbrich claims that while there would be some progressivity under a flat tax system, there would be much less than under the current system. In addition, she claims that three tax incentives that are important to middle-class families would be eliminated under a flat tax system. She concludes that the simplicity of the flat tax is not reason enough to adopt it. Ulbrich is a senior scholar at the Strom Thurmond Institute of Government and Public Affairs of Clemson University.

As you read, consider the following questions:

1. According to the author, the top tax rate on incomes over $200,000 was what percentage late in World War II?

2. Ulbrich claims that the flat tax is not actually flat for what reason?

Holley Ulbrich, "Income Tax Day—Flat and Simple, or Fair and Complicated?" Strom Thurmond Institute, 2010. www.strom.clemson.edu. Reproduced by permission.

3. Fringe benefits from employers typically cost about what percentage of wages and salaries, according to Ulbrich?

April 15th is the deadline for filing your federal tax return, and in many states, your state tax return. Unlike most of the holidays in this series of essays, income tax day is not related to a historical event or the turning of the seasons. It's just an arbitrary day chosen by the federal government as a deadline—late enough in the year so that people have a chance to collect the documents and fill out the forms for the year that ended 3-1/2 months ago, early enough so that the government has some revenue for the last half of the fiscal year that ends on October 1st.

Historical Tax Rates

Americans have been paying federal income taxes since the 16th amendment to the Constitution was ratified in 1913. The original income tax had marginal rates ranging from one percent on the first $20,000 of taxable income to seven percent on income over $500,000. The revenue needs of World War I quickly drove the top bracket rate up to 67% on incomes over $2 million. The top bracket rate dropped to 25% in the 1920s, only to rise again during the Great Depression. By late in World War II, the top rate was 94% on incomes over $200,000. The top bracket rate dropped to 91% after the war and stayed there until 1964, then to 70% until 1982, when it fell again to 50%. Today, the maximum marginal rate is 35%.

But the marginal or top bracket tax rate is not even close to the amount of tax paid as a percent of income. In 2010, for example, that top rate of 35% only applied to taxable income (after deductions and exemptions) over $373,650. Dollars of taxable income under $373,650 were subject to marginal rates ranging from 10% to 33%. After exemptions, deductions, credits, and applying lower rates to the first parts of income, the average American paid 12.7% of gross income in federal income taxes in 2007.

The Flat Tax Proposal

It's true that the tax code is long and complicated. It's also true that, for the vast majority of taxpayers, it's not that complicated. Families who don't itemize or claim credits for buying new houses or making their existing homes more energy efficient can file quickly and easily. Tax preparers and tax preparation software have also simplified the task of filling out tax returns. Nevertheless, there is a movement to vastly simplify the federal income tax code to the point where it can be filed on a postcard. That proposal is called the flat tax. Economist Alvin Rabushka is credited with developing the idea, which has been reflected in a variety of proposals and takes some responsibility for various tax simplifications and rate reductions.

Strictly speaking, the proposed flat tax is not flat. It exempts some floor amount of income per household and taxes the rest of income at a single flat rate. For a poor household, that exempt amount may be 80% or 90% of income, so the flat rate would only apply to a small part of income. For a wealthy household, that same exempt amount would be a much smaller share of total income, so the flat rate would apply to most of income. As a result, the poor household would be paying a much lower percentage of total income in taxes than the rich household. So even a flat tax is progressive, although it would be much less progressive than our current structure with rates ranging from 10% to 35%. In an overall state and local revenue system with lots of regressive taxes that hit poor and middle income households harder, there's something to be said for a fairly progressive federal income tax as a balancing factor. But perhaps simplification is worth giving up that benefit of our present system?

Downsides of the Flat Tax

Not necessarily. There's one more important complication in going to flat and simple. We would have to give up some cherished deductions and credits. For middle income households, there are three important tax incentives (or what economists call tax expenditures) that would be affected. One is the deduction for mortgage interest and property taxes on their homes. Most households figure those deductions into deciding how much home they can afford to buy. Suddenly the deduction is gone! Middle and upper income households also take the tax deduction into account when they make charitable contributions. The higher your marginal rate, the less it costs you to give another dollar to charity. Under the flat tax, the charitable deduction would be gone. it's hard to know what the impact would be on charities ranging from churches and colleges to soup kitchens and museums.

The biggest hit for middle income households, however, would come in employer-provided fringe benefits, of which the largest are health insurance and pension contributions. Fringe benefits typically cost about 30% of wages and salaries, so all of a sudden the federal government would think you were earning 30% more for tax purposes. People also save in tax exempt forms that would no longer enjoy that tax privilege. A flat tax would discourage saving for retirement and providing health insurance.

The income tax is complicated for a number of reasons. Certainly it is full of loopholes and privileges granted to particular firms and individuals. But it does offset some of the other regressive taxes in the system. And it's also a great way for the government to encourage us to do things we should be doing anyway—saving for retirement, reducing our carbon footprint, investing in our homes, contributing to charity. So before we join the tax protestors and demand that the income tax be simplified, we need to take a look at our own tax forms and think about what is our fair share to pay and what good things we did just because the tax code was encouraging us to do the right thing.

| "Americans are better off under the Fair-
| Tax."

A Single Rate, Federal Sales Tax Is the Best Tax System

Americans For Fair Taxation

In the following viewpoint, the organization Americans For Fair Taxation argues that the current tax system needs to be replaced by what the author calls a "FairTax" system—a single rate, federal sales tax. The author contends that the FairTax would ensure greater fairness than the current system, be simpler, and be more efficient in collecting taxes. In addition, Americans For Fair Taxation claims that replacing the current tax system with a federal sales tax would result in a healthier economy. Americans For Fair Taxation is a nonprofit organization dedicated to fully replacing the US federal income tax system with a national sales tax.

As you read, consider the following questions:

1. The author proposes that under the FairTax Plan what taxes would be repealed?

Americans For Fair Taxation, "The FairTax: Good for Taxpayers, Good for Business, Good for the Economy," pp.1–6, 2011. www.fairtax.org. Reproduced by permission.

2. According to the author, under the FairTax a family of four earning $29,420 would pay how much in federal taxes?

3. Americans for Fair Taxation claims that the current tax code, regulations covering implementation, and court rulings fill how many pages?

The national debate over taxation is shifting from the question of *whether* to alter our current tax system to the question of *how* to alter it. Today, polls indicate that a large majority of Americans are extremely frustrated with the current federal income tax system. The income tax discourages personal savings and investments by taxing capital gains, dividends, and interest earned. Wage earners struggle under the burden of a very regressive payroll tax. The income tax is complex—so complex that no one, not even the experts, truly understands it. Moreover, for the tax to be enforced, the taxpayer must sacrifice significant privacy. As a result, our citizens are governed by needlessly burdensome tax laws that they cannot understand and that are intrusive, complex, costly, and often invisible.

The tremendous undertaking of replacing the income tax requires the American people to put aside partisan politics to arrive at a consensus on how our government should tax its citizens. Any new system of taxation must fairly and efficiently distribute the burden of funding our government, promote economic growth, present less of a compliance burden, and offer every American better economic opportunity.

Americans For Fair Taxation (FairTax.org), a non-profit, non-partisan organization, believes that replacing the current tax system with a single rate, federal sales tax levied on all new goods and services with no exceptions or exclusions, best meets this challenge. Research has shown that the FairTax is a fair and progressive system of taxation that increases economic growth, investment, capital formation, and the creation of jobs and savings.[1]

The FairTax plan

The FairTax Plan involves three specific actions:

- Passage of legislation that repeals the income tax, the payroll tax in its entirety, the estate tax, the gift tax, the capital gains tax, the alternative minimum tax, the self-employment tax, and the corporate tax.

- Passage of legislation that installs a single rate, national sales tax on all new goods and services at the point of final purchase for consumption, and that provides for a universal rebate in an amount equal to the sales tax on essential goods and services up to poverty level spending.

- Adoption of a constitutional amendment to repeal the 16th Amendment and to prohibit income taxes. The FairTax will sunset if the 16th Amendment has not been repealed within seven years following enactment, preventing the possibility of having both the income tax and a national sales tax.

The FairTax has been introduced as "The Fair Tax Act of 2011" in the 112th Congress (H.R. 25 in the House of Representatives and S. 13 in the Senate).[2]

Fairness

Throughout the history of our country, our citizens and government have had an objective to increase every American's chance to achieve economic independence by providing greater opportunities to share in our country's growth and prosperity. The FairTax helps us achieve this goal. Americans are better off under the FairTax. Although every taxpayer is subject to the same sales tax rate with no exceptions or exclusions, those least able to share in the cost of government will carry no federal tax burden at all.[3] Under the current system, the more your income is derived from wages, the more you are affected by payroll taxes. In addition, under the FairTax, no one will pay tax on the cost of essential purchases, and those who demonstrate their greater ability to pay by consuming more, will pay more taxes.[4]

Table 1 [not shown, visit www.fairtax.org to view table] shows that a sample family of four with a poverty level income of $29,4205 has an effective federal tax rate of -2.7 percent of their gross income, when the Earned Income Credit of $3,350 is taken into account. A sample family earning $58,840 pays 14.5 percent of their gross income in federal taxes. Under the FairTax, the family of four earning $29,420[5] (spending all of their income) pays zero federal taxes (after the prebate), and the same family of four earning and spending $58,840 pays an effective tax rate of only 11.5 percent tax on their taxable purchases.

However, this is not the whole picture. While payroll taxes are levied equally between employers and employees, it is the broad consensus among economists, including those at the Congressional Budget Office and the Joint Committee on Taxation, that it is really the *employee* that bears the burden of the *employer* portions of Social Security and Medicare payroll taxes, and Federal Unemployment Taxes through *lower wages than would otherwise be paid*.[6] On this basis, the true burden of the current federal income tax system on taxpayers becomes even more dramatic.

Given that the employer share of payroll taxes in actuality reflects a reduction of the employee's potential wages, we can determine the "actual" tax burden as shown in Table 2 [not shown, visit www.fairtax.org to view table].

First, we increase the gross family income amounts from Table 1[not shown, visit www.fairtax.org to view table] by the amount of employer payroll taxes (Federal Unemployment Tax, Social Security and Medicare). In the first example, employer taxes of $434 (FUT), $1,824 (SS), and $427 (Med) are added to the employee's income of $29,420 to obtain a "potential" income of $32,105. The total taxes paid are then compared to the total potential income to determine the actual tax burden which in this case is 5.9 percent ($1,888 divided by $32,105).[7] For the family with "potential" income of $63,775 the effective tax rate jumps dramatically to 21.1 percent reflecting that their income exceeds the maximum to qualify for the Earned Income Tax Credit.

The FairTax amount is calculated by multiplying the rate of 23 percent times family income, assuming that all income is spent. This amount is divided by income to yield an effective tax rate. For comparable income levels, the FairTax effective tax rate is substantially less than under the current system. In the case of the family with income of $32,105, the effective rate is only 1.9 percent. The tax rate for the $63,775 income level jumps to 12.4 percent but that is still much less than the 21.1 percent rate for the current tax system. The results show the comparative advantage of the FairTax over the total tax burden paid by employees today. It further illustrates the "true" progressive nature of the FairTax compared to the current system which imposes the same effective tax rate of 21.1 percent on a family with income of $63,775 as that experienced by a family with income of $126,442. This occurs as a result of the wage base cap of $106,800 for Social Security taxes.

Our current tax system is also unfair because it is highly responsive to political influence on behalf of special interest groups. Average taxpayers without the means or organization to influence tax policy are at a clear disadvantage. The inextricable relationship between the tax code and lobbyists is evidenced by the fact that more than half of Washington lobbyists are registered on tax matters. Under the FairTax, there are no exceptions and there are no exclusions—there are no loopholes to be exploited by special interests. Under the FairTax, all taxpayers have an equal voice.

Simplicity

A fundamental notion of fairness is that citizens should be able to comprehend the laws that affect them. However, current tax law is beyond the comprehension of most taxpayers, including many of those who devote their entire professional lives to it. In the long-running experiment of the income tax, it is fairly well demonstrated that it is the nature of the income tax as a hidden tax that breeds complexity. The constantly growing complexity of our tax system is part of a trend that began in 1913 and has only accelerated with the nearly perennial enactment of new tax legislation with 4,428 changes to the tax code in just the last decade. In 2010 alone there were 579 changes; more than one per day![8] The continuous tinkering with the tax code has resulted in tripling the length of the tax code, now a mind-boggling 3.8 million words.[9] The combined federal income tax code, regulations, and IRS rulings have grown from 14,000 pages in 1954 to 72,536 pages by 2011—an increase of 518 percent.[10]

The FairTax is simple: One single rate, with no exceptions and no exclusions, collected at the point of purchase. The simplicity of the FairTax means that tax planning is now within the reach of the ordinary taxpayer, who can choose when and whether to pay federal taxes by deciding when to make purchases and whether to buy new or used products.

Efficiency

In addition to the taxes on income that we pay, we also pay the cost of payroll and corporate taxes that are embedded in every product that we purchase. Businesses pass their costs on to consumers in the form of higher prices. But the burden to the consumer doesn't stop there. We also pay for the cost of complying with the tax code. So complicated has the income tax system become that an analysis of IRS data by the Taxpayer Advocate Service estimates that individual taxpayers and businesses spend 6.1 billion hours each year complying with the filing requirements of the Internal Revenue Code. The Tax Foundation estimated compliance costs to exceed $265 billion or 3.1 percent of the Gross Domestic Product.11 That is equivalent to nearly a $1,000 tax on every American.

Massive amounts of our national wealth are consumed merely by measuring, tracking, sheltering, documenting, and filing our annual income. The twin burdens of time and money required for record keeping, tax form preparation, calculating and funding estimated payment schedules, and tracking income and expenses are eliminated by the FairTax. The FairTax generates the same amount of revenue as the current tax system, but at a much lower cost. The number of tax filers drops from 164.6 million[12] to an estimated 30 million, an 81 percent reduction. Compliance costs under the FairTax are expected to fall by 85 to 90 percent from their current level.

Economic Impact

Slow economic growth and economic stagnation have an adverse impact on low wage earners. These families are more likely to lose their jobs, are less likely to have the resources to weather bad economic times, and are more in need of the initial employment opportunities that a dynamic, growing economy provides. The income tax retards economic performance by creating a significant bias against saving and investment through double, triple, and even quadruple taxation.

Under the FairTax, what you earn is what you take home. Americans are able to save more and invest more. Education tuition and job training are treated as investment in human capital and are not taxed, enabling individuals to invest in their skills as well. The FairTax dramatically increases investment levels compared to levels that would have been achieved under the current income tax system.[13] Increased savings will stimulate investment and productivity and the economy will grow more rapidly, creating demand for workers and improving job opportunities. Because taxes on capital are removed, foreign capital will flow into the United States, creating businesses and jobs. U.S. products competing abroad are free of the hidden costs of taxation while the FairTax is collected on foreign products sold in the United States. Virtually all economic models project a much healthier economy under a broad-based consumption tax such as the FairTax.

Summary

The ever-increasing taxpayer demand for a less intrusive system of taxation is building daily. The FairTax delivers these benefits to the American people, and more—more government accountability for taxpayer dollars, the elimination of individual tax returns, a tax system which is transparent and less susceptible to being manipulated by special interests, and perhaps most importantly, a tax system that encourages economic growth and job creation.

What Is the FairTax Plan?

The FairTax Plan is a comprehensive proposal that replaces all federal income and payroll taxes with an integrated approach including a progressive national retail sales tax, a rebate to ensure no American pays federal taxes on spending up to the poverty level, dollar-for-dollar federal revenue replacement, and, through companion legislation, repeal of the 16th Amendment. This nonpartisan legislation (HR 25/S 13) abolishes all federal personal, gift, estate, capital gains, alternative minimum, Social Security, Medicare, self-employment, and corporate taxes and replaces them with one simple, visible, federal retail sales tax—collected by existing state sales tax authorities. The FairTax taxes us only on what we choose to spend, not on what we earn. It does not raise any more or less revenue; it is designed to be revenue neutral. The FairTax is a fair, efficient, transparent, and intelligent solution to the frustration and inequity of our current tax system.

What Is Americans For Fair Taxation (FairTax.org)?

FairTax.org is a nonprofit, nonpartisan, grassroots organization dedicated to replacing the current tax system. The organization has hundreds of thousands of members and volunteers nationwide. Its plan supports sound economic research, education of citizens and community leaders, and grassroots mobilization efforts. For more information visit the Web page: www.FairTax.org or call 1-800-FAIRTAX.

Notes

1. Kotlikoff, Laurence J. and Sabine Jokisch, "Simulating the Dynamic Macroeconomic and Microeconomic Effects of the FairTax," *National Tax Journal*, June 2007; David G. Tuerck, et.al., "The Economic Effects of the FairTax: Results from the Beacon Hill Institute CGE Model," The Beacon Hill Institute at Suffolk University, February 2007; Arduin, Laffer & Moore Econometrics, A Macroeconomic Analysis of the FairTax Proposal, June, 2006; David G. Tuerck, Jonathan Haughton, Paul Bachman, and Alfonso Sanchez-Penalver, "A Comparison of the FairTax Base and Rate with Other National Tax Reform Proposals," The Beacon Hill Institute at Suffolk University, February, 2007; Laurence J. Kotlikoff, and David G. Tuerck, *et. al.*, "Taxing Sales under the FairTax: What Rate Works?" *Tax Notes*, November 13, 2006. These papers are available at www.fairtax.org/AboutTheFairTax/ResearchPapers.

2. H.R. 25 is sponsored by Congressman Rob Woodall, with 55 co-sponsors and S. 13 by Senator Saxby Chambliss with 5 co-sponsors as of March 3, 2011.

3. Kotlikoff, Laurence J. and David Rapson, "Comparing Average and Marginal Tax Rates under the FairTax and the Current System of Federal Taxation," NBER Working Paper No. 12533, revised October 2006; Kahn, Joseph, "Examining a

Change to a National Retail Sales Tax Regime: Impact on Households," Decisions and Ethics Center, Stanford University, November, 1996.

4. The analysis shown in Tables 1 and 2 does not include the one year (2011) payroll tax reduction for employees.

5. This income level is derived from the poverty level guideline for a family of four, two adults, two children. See Federal Register, Vol. 76, No. 13, Jan. 20, 2011.

6. See Congressional Budget Office, "Historical Effective Federal Tax Rates, 1979-2006," April 2009 and Joint Committee on Taxation, "Overview of Present Law and Economic Analysis Relating to Marginal Tax Rates and the President's Individual Income Tax Rate Proposals," March 6, 2001.

7. (-$3,048) + $434 + (2 x $1,824) + (2 x 427) = $1,888.

8. Taxpayer Advocate Service, 2010 Annual Report to Congress, "The Time for Tax Reform is Now," Dec. 31, 2010, p. 4.

9. See above.

10. As measured by the number of pages in the 2011 CCH Standard Federal Tax Reporter.

11. Moody, J. Scott, Wendy P. Warcholik, and Scott A. Hodge, "The Rising Cost of Complying with the Federal Income Tax," Tax Foundation, Special Report No. 138, December 2005.

12. 2009 IRS Databook.

13. Kotlikoff, Laurence J. and Sabine Jokisch, "Simulating the Dynamic Macroeconomic and Microeconomic Effects of the FairTax," *National Tax Journal*, June 2007; David G. Tuerck, et.al., "The Economic Effects of the FairTax: Results from the Beacon Hill Institute CGE Model," The Beacon Hill Institute at Suffolk University, February 2007.

"Since the FairTax is a tax reform proposal instead of a tax reduction proposal, it merely changes the way that
taxes are collected."

A Single Rate, Federal Sales Tax Is Not the Best System

Laurence M. Vance

In the following viewpoint, Laurence M. Vance argues that the proposal to implement a single rate, federal sales tax is misguided. Vance contends that there are numerous misconceptions of the so-called FairTax plan, including the beliefs that the plan will eliminate all other taxes or lower the overall tax burden. Vance claims there is no reason to believe that the FairTax would be any simpler than the current system and concludes that a reduction in taxes—not a new system—is the solution. Vance is a writer and an adjunct instructor in accounting at Pensacola Junior College in Florida.

As you read, consider the following questions:

1. What taxes does Vance claim would not be eliminated by the FairTax?

Laurence M. Vance, "There Is Still No Such Thing as a Fair Tax," Ludwig von Mises Institute, May 2008. Reproduced by permission.

2. What two things are exempted from taxation under the FairTax plan, according to Vance?

3. According to the author, what is the fundamental problem about taxes?

The FairTax is a revenue-neutral consumption tax in the form of a national retail sales tax on all new goods and services that is designed to replace *most* federal taxes: personal income taxes, corporate income taxes, estate taxes, gift taxes, unemployment taxes, alternative minimum taxes, capital gains taxes, Social Security taxes, and Medicare taxes.

Misconceptions About the FairTax

Although it seems like the price we would have to pay for the elimination of these taxes is higher prices on all new goods and services because of the imposition of a high sales tax, FairTax proponents claim that the removal of embedded taxes—the tax burdens of businesses that contribute to the overall cost of products—will result in the prices of goods and services falling by enough to offset the amount of the FairTax imposed. In addition to this dubious conclusion, there are some misconceptions about the FairTax that should be pointed out.

The FairTax does not eliminate all taxes. It does not eliminate tariffs on imported goods, federal excise taxes on products like gasoline and tobacco, special taxes on things like telephone service and airline tickets, or any state and local sales, gasoline, or hotel taxes.

The FairTax does not lower the overall tax burden. Since it is revenue neutral, the total amount of taxes the federal government extracts from the citizens of the United States would be the same as it is now.

The FairTax does not eliminate the IRS [Internal Revenue Service]. Calling the IRS by another name, and redirecting its mission, is hardly eliminating it. Just as the income tax would be replaced by the FairTax, so the IRS would be replaced by the "Sales Tax Bureau" in the Treasury Department. True, there would be no more audits, no more tax forms, no more April 15, and no more compliance costs *for individuals*, but there would be an increase in these things *for businesses*.

The FairTax does not eliminate the Sixteenth Amendment. To repeal the Sixteenth Amendment would require a constitutional amendment to that effect, as the Twenty-First Amendment repealed the Eighteenth. Not only is there no guarantee that Congress would propose such an amendment, it would still have to be sent to the states and approved by three-fourths of them.

Even if the prices of goods and services fall after the change to the FairTax system, with the sale of new homes and cars being taxed, as well as services from heart surgeries down to haircuts, the FairTax would result in a tremendous change in American society. Is it worth expending so much effort on changing *the way* the federal government collects taxes instead of changing *the amount* that the federal government collects in taxes? This is a question that doesn't even have to be answered since the stated rate of the FairTax is too low to achieve revenue neutrality and the amount by which prices would fall under a FairTax system has been grossly exaggerated.

The FairTax Tax Code

FairTax proponents are naïve about what would happen to their system once it was adopted. What makes them think that Congress wouldn't turn the FairTax into a monstrosity just as hideous as the current tax code?

The original tax code was, like the FairTax, short and simple. However, it didn't take long for Congress to turn it into the lengthy, complex, unjust system that it is today. What makes FairTax supporters think that Congress won't begin to tweak the FairTax as soon as it goes into effect?

The rate of any of the three components of the FairTax (the general revenue rate; the old-age, survivors and disability insurance rate; and the hospital rate) could be raised at any time. The spiraling costs of Social Security and Medicare, as well as the coming depletion of the "surplus" in their trust funds, guarantees that the FairTax rate will certainly have to be raised. The insolvency of Medicare has been compounded, of course, by one of the greatest expansions of the welfare state since the Great Society, the Medicare Prescription Drug and Modernization Act of 2003—which Congressman [and FairTax proponent John] Linder voted for.

The only things currently exempted from the FairTax are tuition and job-related training courses. The demand to expand this exemption to food will certainly be the first and the loudest that we hear. And since we know how unpredictable and irrational Congress is, there is no telling what will come next. Then it will be exemptions on *certain* goods and services if they are used for *certain* purposes or purchased by *certain* types of companies.

The FairTax system includes a monthly payment from the federal government given to all households called a "prebate" that reimburses each household for the national sales tax paid on basic necessities. The elimination of this prebate for the rich and upper-income taxpayers will be one of the first changes made to the FairTax plan. A means test will certainly follow. Since the amount of the prebate is tied to the annually adjusted government poverty level, it will go up every year for everyone. And we can count on pressure to raise the prebate by a greater amount for certain income groups like seniors on fixed incomes, the poor with low incomes, anyone receiving public assistance, anyone making the minimum wage, or anyone who would have qualified for the earned income credit under the old income tax system.

The Fundamental Problem

Additionally, what makes FairTax advocates think that we won't end up with both a federal *sales* tax and a federal *income* tax? Most countries with a VAT [value-added tax] also have an income tax. Adopting the FairTax doesn't mean that the income tax couldn't be reimposed. Congress might simply decide to resurrect the income tax because it is not politically expedient to raise the rate of the FairTax. This could be implemented by lowering the rate of the FairTax, reinstituting the income tax, and then claiming that the combination of the two was revenue neutral. And even if the Sixteenth Amendment were repealed, there is nothing preventing Congress from implementing some form of an income tax, as the Foundation for Economic Education's Sheldon Richman has recently explained in great detail. . . .

As I have emphasized every time I have written about taxes, the fundamental problem is taxation itself, not the tax code. Yes, the tax code is too complex, too intrusive, and too long. Yes, compliance costs are too high. Yes, the tax code punishes success. But since the FairTax is a tax *reform* proposal instead of a tax *reduction* proposal, it merely changes the way that taxes are collected. With the federal budget now topping $3 trillion, and the national debt fast approaching $10 trillion, the need of the hour is clearly to rein in government spending, not change the way the government raises its revenue—or give it more revenue as the FairTax would do. "The real issue," as Congressman Ron Paul has so often said, "is total spending by government, not tax reform."

Taxes should be repealed or reduced, not replaced or reformed. Advocates of liberty and less government should focus not on *fairness* but on *lowness*.

> *"A system that fails to tax those most able to pay creates a spending problem."*

The Tax System Should Be More Progressive

Robin Blackburn

In the following viewpoint, Robin Blackburn argues that the current US tax system should be made more progressive. Blackburn contends that the wealthy currently escape taxation by holding their wealth in shares of corporations, leaving the middle class to shoulder too much of the tax burden. He concludes that the best solution is to impose a share levy that would mainly affect the very rich. Blackburn is professor of sociology at the University of Essex in the United Kingdom, and he is the author of Age Shock and Pension Power: How Finance Is Failing Us.

As you read, consider the following questions:

1. According to Blackburn, what defines an aristocrat today?

2. The author claims that corporations now supply what percentage of the federal revenue?

Robin Blackburn, "How to Tax the Rich—And Live Happily Ever After," *Dissent*, Summer 2007. Reproduced by permission.

3. According to Blackburn, a 10 percent share/partnership levy would have raised how much money in 2005?

Sharpening inequality, rocketing "financial partnership" income, and obscene levels of executive "compensation" make all the more unacceptable the accompanying massacre of job-related entitlements to health care and pensions. Mounting foreclosures, bankruptcies, and threats to employment itself have led to a deepening and widespread sense of insecurity. Many of these insecurities affect the middle class as much as the poor.

The Need for Funding

One response has been outbreaks of economic populism. Unfortunately, some populists aim at the wrong target and fail to press the most important measures of redress. For example, some attack Hispanics rather than a tax system that the corporations and the rich evade almost at will. A system that fails to tax those most able to pay creates a spending problem.

The Democrats talk about permanently raising the Alternative Minimum Tax (AMT) so that it will not apply to households earning less than $200,000 or $250,000 a year. AMT is now gnawing away at medium-earning households, many of them in states that the Democrats have to win. But if AMT is to go, or its threshold be raised permanently, where will the nearly trillion dollars of taxes it raises come from?

The Democrats' spending plans are too modest, but they still require more, not less, public revenue. Thus Robert Rubin, the former treasury secretary, has warned that Democratic spending promises cannot be met by an already overburdened public purse. Yet there are many good causes out there that demand funding—health care insurance, lower college tuition fees, more research and development, better pension funding, and protection against climate change, to mention just a few.

Of course, withdrawal from Iraq could save the treasury hundreds of billions of dollars. But much of the trillion-dollar cost has already been incurred, so even a rapid withdrawal would still leave a sizable spending gap. What is really needed are taxes that cannot be easily evaded and that target the new financial aristocracy, especially hedge fund managers and the general partners in private equity outfits.

Tax Exemption for the Rich

What defines an aristocrat today, as in the France of the ancien régime, is not blue blood but privileged exemption from the ordinary workings of the law and of the tax system. About five hundred executives and financial officers have ended up in jail over the last few years. But despite an extraordinary raft of financial scams, the number of Wall Street professionals who have ended up behind bars can be counted on the fingers of one hand (and those against whom prosecutions are pending are almost all small fry). Likewise, almost nine times as many Wall Street fund managers earned more than a hundred million dollars a year in 2006 as public company chief executive officers. Moreover, the princes of private equity will typically pay tax on much of their declared capital gains at a 15 percent rate, while chief executive officers will find much of their income caught by the 35 percent rate.

The tax debate should really be about taxing the haves, not squeezing the have-nots. Taxes on middle-class earners and spenders currently raise a lot of cash because this population has few ways of evading them. Taxes on the rich are routinely evaded. In the 2004 campaign, George W. Bush candidly explained that it was a waste of time simply raising nominal tax rates on the rich because they will avoid them, as "they have accountants to make sure of that."

In fact, the super-rich don't even have to practice avoidance to pay little tax. [Billionaire] Warren Buffett doesn't use any tax planning, yet discovered that the proportion of his income taken by tax and Social Security payments was lower than that of anyone else in his Omaha [Neb.] office. A telltale sign of corporate tax avoidance showed up in a recent report from the Internal Revenue Service. It pointed out that U.S. companies that reported $707 billion in profit to Wall Street in 2004 scaled that back to $523 billion when submitting their tax returns. In the boom years 1996–2000, 61 percent of U.S. companies paid no federal income tax. And those that did pay tax on overseas profits reduced the effective tax rate from 24 percent to 20 percent. Boston Consulting Group estimates that offshore private banking assets now total almost six trillion dollars.

But the real steal is the booty carried home by private equity general partners. These gentry raise cash from investors, including pension funds, using it to acquire public companies that they believe to be undervalued. They take the company private and carry out a financial reorganization that typically involves selling property and then leasing it back, shrinking employee entitlements, and taking out huge loans. They pay no tax on the interest accruing on these loans. Capital gains and dividends pay tax at lower rates than income. The general partner will charge a fee of 2 percent on the funds under management and also claim—in the standard "two and twenty" formula—20 percent of the "carried interest," or gross profit on the sale of the reorganized company.

Restoring Progressivity to the Tax System

Globalization and sophisticated tax avoidance have greatly weakened progressive taxation, but we do not have to give in to fatalism and despair. The overall tax take in most advanced countries is still pretty high—a quarter or a third, or more, of gross domestic products. Too much of it is paid by the struggling middle class and the low paid. It doesn't have to be like this. The rich prefer to live in countries that are law-abiding, safe, and prosperous. The tax rates in the Cayman Islands, Belize, or Liberia may be great, but do the rich want to live there? As a result, even Wall Street bankers find themselves paying some taxes on their bonuses. Likewise, hedge fund managers park their compensation offshore, but when they need to retrieve it they will have to pay some tax.

An administration that meant business could raise the effective tax rate. Without doubt global competition and "financialization"—techniques for swapping and disguising income streams or assets—have given special advantage to the high rollers. They have undermined redistribution via taxes at a time when inequality abounds and the corporate world regards employee welfare as no longer its concern. Corporations used to supply 20 percent of federal revenue, now the figure is only 4 percent. They used to be proud of their health and retirement programs; now they are eager to be rid of them. In effect it is the owners of the corporations—large-scale shareholders and private equity partnerships—who gain. One half of all corporate stock is owned by the richest one percent of the population—those with incomes over one million dollars a year.

So the $64-billion question is how to restore progressivity and how to make the corporations and those who own them contribute at a more serious rate.

There is no harm in removing the income tax cut for the wealthy or in reprieving the estates duty or "death tax." Just don't expect to raise more than a trickle by so doing. The yield of such taxes is always reduced by loopholes. Try to plug these, but be aware that many are there to ensure that the tax doesn't hit small business, struggling professionals, and the middle class. In fact, there is no country in the world where estate duties have raised serious sums, partly because they can be anticipated and partly because legislators don't want to penalize the widows of farmers, shopkeepers and home owners.

Tax Options

The familiar taxes are the most easily avoided, so why not try something new? If legislators could throw off their fear of tax innovation, what could they do?

Green taxes—aimed at high carbon producers, say—could produce useful revenue. However, if the tax is really effective at discouraging pollution then it won't raise much revenue; it also may not be progressive, in that the rich will be better placed to minimize their exposure. Issuing each citizen with tradable carbon quotas is likely to be more effective in reducing emissions but won't raise revenues for general purposes. In any case, the money raised from green charges should probably be reserved to defray the heavy costs of climate change.

Taxing property rather than income offers interesting possibilities. The idea of taxing increases in commercial land values is not at all new—it was a favorite of [American economist] Henry George more than a century ago—but is still worth exploring. Commercial land increases in value either because of public investments (on infrastructure and social facilities) or a general increase in national prosperity. The pure rent that accrues to commercial property owners is thus a windfall profit that can be heavily taxed without harmful effect of any sort—and the property itself is visible, making evasion difficult or impossible. A number of towns in Pennsylvania, including Harrisburg, the state capital, have raised serious sums in this way. However, if such a land tax is not addressed at a federal level, different jurisdictions may be tempted to compete with one another by offering lower rates; the latter does not completely remove the case for raising taxes on commercial land but it could limit the yield.

The Real Treasure

In fairy tales, the real treasure is guarded by a scary monster. The same goes for tax policy. The real treasure is locked up in the holdings of the richest 1 percent who, as noted above, own half of all shares. At present those who own the home they live in pay annual property taxes, but the rich who own a pile of shares or partnership rights pay nothing. Capital gains tax is not paid at regular intervals but only when a share is sold.

The monster preventing politicians and wonks from thinking about taxing shares is the knowledge that—however concentrated shareholding wealth may be—it is also sufficiently widely held to make trespassing upon it a minefield. After all, one half of all Americans own shares—and the other half dreams of doing so.

Still, the credibility of the New York Stock Exchange is as compromised as that of the U.S. Congress. Scandals have revealed the multiple ways in which chief executive officers and money managers have looted the assets entrusted to them to manage. The really rich have access to the hedge funds that can prevent this, but small and medium investors have been fleeced repeatedly by money managers. Eliot Spitzer's thumping victory as New York governor showed that most voters like a tough approach to the financial and corporate skimmers.

The Share Levy Solution

The indispensable task of taxing share-holding wealth could best be approached by a share levy. This would require every public corporation to issue shares equivalent to 10 percent of its profits each year. The effect would be a mild dilution of share value—equivalent to about 0.68 percent of share value each year. In recent years the dilution effect of stock options and of takeovers has often been greater than this.

What could be done with the fruits of a share levy? And what could be done to appease those who are, or would like to be, small investors? The share-levy proceeds could be channeled to a regional network of reserve social funds, and every

Restoring Progressive Taxation

Americans don't want to blow up our tax system and start over. Instead, we want to restore the values of progressive taxation that have historically guided U.S. tax policy. The federal income tax—the cornerstone of the tax code—needs to be restructured, simplified, and broadened. This means eliminating loopholes for corporations and wealthy individuals, simplifying the rate structure, and reversing the trend of unfairly lower tax rates on the capital income of the wealthiest Americans.

John S. Irons and John Podesta,
"A Tax Plan for Progressives," American Prospect, June 2005.

citizen could be given a say in how they were used. Such a network might be linked to state-level trust funds and could be monitored by the regional Federal Reserve Banks.

The share levy would have the advantage that it would not take a toll—as does corporation taxation—from the cash flow of the company. The latter weakens investment and can cut jobs. The network should also be obliged to hold the shares indefinitely, not to sell them. The funds would be held to generate future revenue from dividend income. On the whole, dividends are less volatile than either share prices or profits, so the future yield could be estimated.

A further advantage is that the levy would mildly tax shares wherever they were held. Shares held in a tax haven would not escape dilution. And if assessing the levy purely on net profit was thought too trusting, then it could be assessed on gross profit or even as a percentage of total market value.

The companies owned by private equity partnerships could also be taxed more fairly. The levy would take the form of notional partnership rights in the "carried interest." It would also be possible to reduce the tax advantage applying to interest payments and provide that interest payments paid to any stringently defined related party be subject to taxation. Germany and Denmark have already embarked on this. Those interested in such possibilities would do well to skip the standard literature put out by tame partnership tax jocks and turn instead to papers submitted to the "Junior Tax Scholars Conference".

Although the allocation of notional partnership rights to the taxing authority will also help to curb financial privilege, the latter is also defended by a scary monster. The offsetting of interest against tax benefits both the partner in a private equity deal and the modest home owner paying off a mortgage. Indeed, the very structure of the partnership form was designed to favor the mom-and-pop store or small business, yet has ended up awarding huge tax breaks to the mega-wealthy. It would not be difficult to retain the favorable treatment for the small-business and the home owner while removing it for large-scale investment.

Safeguarding Legitimate Interests

However, there is one type of large investor whose interests would be worth safeguarding, those of bona fide pension funds and endowments. The latter have taken to investing huge sums in private equity in recent years. Although some have done well, the gains of these "limited partner" investors as a whole are heavily eroded by the general partners' "two and twenty" charging formula. It would probably be best for genuine pension funds to shun these expensive investment opportunities and instead band together and take over the general partner function. Recently, the Ontario Teachers' plan has mounted a $25 billion bid for Bell Canada, while the United Kingdom's Wellcome Trust backed an $18 billion bid for Boots Alliance, a retail chain. The April 12, 2007, headline put on this story by the *Financial Times* says it all: "Much Better Returns without the Fees." In each case, the huge funds are perfectly able to hire any needed financial expertise rather than groan under the "two and twenty" burden. However, such ventures would work even better as a species of social entrepreneurship if several large public sector funds went together. Please note that the logic here is very different from an Employee Self-Ownership Plan (ESOP), which concentrates employee risk; indeed, unscrupulous private equity promoters have spotted the opportunity and have adapted such plans to their own leveraged buy-out strategies.

By my calculations, a 10 percent share/partnership levy would have raised $141.7 billion in 2005, which, if reinvested over a twenty-seven-year period, would be worth $10.9 trillion in 2033, generating annual income of around $400 billion, equivalent to the entirety of today's Social Security program or to 2 percent of future GDP [gross domestic product].

If all citizens had rights in this fund, then this might somewhat allay the small investor's fears. But something more would have to be offered. It would be possible to give a rebate to all whose holdings were in an approved retirement or health care insurance fund. It would also be possible to charge the reserve fund network with using its growing stake in corporations to ensure good governance. The funds could have a small but expert staff dedicated to monitoring corporate behavior and to redressing the "information asymmetry" between insiders and outsiders.

Use of the Revenue

I have advocated such a levy and fund network as a way of anticipating the heavy future cost of meeting the retirement needs of the baby boomers. But another approach would be to leave open the precise use to which the future revenue would be put. Voters might find quite reassuring the idea that an emergency fund was building up in a way that did not harm today's economy. With the looming shocks in prospect, there is a need for a social reserve fund.

No tax is ever going to be popular, but there is a growing sense of insecurity as risks are shifted onto individuals and families. Last year's elections [2006] showed that most people can tell the difference between their own well being and a buoyant stock market. The share levy would not harm the stock market, but the emergency fund would add an extra standby that could be put toward whatever seemed most urgent in the future. In the meantime, the fund network would promote more enlightened and responsible corporate governance.

The idea of taxing shareholding wealth was first proposed by a Republican, Representative Schuyler Colfax of Indiana. As quoted by W. Elliot Brownlee, he did so in the same speech in 1862 in which he proposed—another first—a progressive tax on income. "I cannot go home and tell my constituents," he declared, "that I voted for a bill that would allow a man, a millionaire, who put his entire property into stock, to be exempt from taxation."

| *"Increasing the progressivity of the tax code threatens to further stifle economic growth."*

The Tax System Should Not Be More Progressive

Curtis S. Dubay

In the following viewpoint, Curtis S. Dubay argues that the federal tax system is already highly progressive and should not be made more progressive by raising taxes for the wealthy. He argues that the wealthy already pay more than their fair share and claims that progressive tax rates stifle economic growth. Dubay concludes that the proposal to make taxes more progressive should be abandoned and that the tax system should actually be made less progressive. Dubay is a senior policy analyst at the Heritage Foundation, where he specializes in tax issues.

As you read, consider the following questions:

1. The author cites a study that shows the top 20 percent of income earners paid what percentage of income taxes in 2006?

Curtis S. Dubay, "Income Tax Will Become More Progressive Under Obama Tax Plan," *Backgrounder No. 2280*, June 1, 2009. Reproduced by permission.

2. According to Dubay, in 2006 a family in the top 1 percent paid how much more in taxes, expressed as a percentage, than did a family in the top 10 percent?

3. The author argues for a tax code that treats taxpayers more equally than the current system, arguing for a system that resembles what?

Today's federal income tax system is highly progressive, with taxpayers at the top of the income spectrum paying higher rates than those in the middle and bottom. The current tax code has six tax brackets with rates ranging from 10 percent (for taxable income up to $16,700) to 35 percent (for taxable income above $372,950 for married couples).

The Increase in Progressivity

President Barack Obama's budget and the budget resolution adopted by Congress would further increase progressivity by raising the tax rates of married couples who earn more than $250,000 a year and singles who earn more than $200,000.

Progressivity discourages hard work, savings, investing, and entrepreneurship. Discouraging these catalysts of economic growth is always counterproductive, but doing so during a severe economic recession is particularly irresponsible.

To make the tax code less progressive and encourage economic growth, Congress should scrap plans to increase tax rates on top earners and instead reduce the number of brackets and lower the rates on those that remain.

A decreasing number of high-income taxpayers are increasingly paying the entire income tax bill. According to the Congressional Budget Office (CBO), the top 20 percent of all income earners paid 86.3 percent of all income taxes in 2006. This was an all-time high and significantly higher than in 2000, before the 2001 and 2003 tax cuts went into effect.

The Statistics Illustrate Progressivity

The drastically progressive income tax code means that high-income taxpayers pay disproportionately higher taxes compared to lower-income taxpayers. Take the average family of four, which qualified for the top quintile of income earners if it earned at least $142,000 in 2006 (the most recent year for which data are available). For 2006, the family paid income taxes of $20,078, and its effective income tax rate—total income taxes paid after deductions and credits divided by income—was 14.1 percent.

A family of four that earned the minimum amount to be included in the second-highest income quintile made $94,800. Its effective income tax rate was 6.0 percent—less than half the top quintile's rate—and its tax bill was $5,688.

Even though the family in the top quintile earned 50 percent more than the family in the second quintile, it paid *253 percent more* in income taxes.

The statistics are even more astounding when one compares a family in the top quintile to families in the middle and lower quintiles. A family of four that earned $64,200, the minimum amount to be classified as middle income, had an effective income tax rate of 3 percent—almost five times lower than the top quintile's rate, and paid $1,926 in income taxes.

The family in the top quintile's income was 122 percent higher than the middle-income family's, but they paid a staggering *943 percent more* in income taxes.

Compared to the bottom 40 percent of income earners, taxpayers in the top quintile pay much higher taxes because taxpayers in the bottom two quintiles generally pay *no income taxes at all*. In fact, they receive payments through the tax code in the form of "refundable credits."

The effective income tax rate for a family of four in the bottom quintile that earned up to $37,800 was -6.6 percent. This means that the average family in this quintile *received* almost $1,300 in income through the tax code.

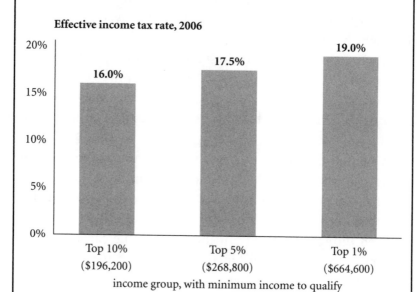

Progressive Tax Rates Increase With Higher Incomes

Figures are for families of four.

Effective income tax rate, 2006

Original Source: Congressional Budget Office, "Data on the Distribution of Federal Taxes and Household Income," April 2009, at *http://www.cbo.gov/publications/collections/taxdistribution.cfm* (May 27, 2009).

TAKEN FROM: Curtis S. Dubay, "Income Tax Will Become More Progressive Under Obama Tax Plan," Backgrounder No. 2280, June 1, 2009.

An average family of four in the second-lowest quintile had an effective income tax rate of -0.8 percent. This family earned up to $64,200 and received an average of $408 of income through the tax code.

Progressivity Knows No End

It is obvious that high-income families pay substantially higher taxes than low and middle-income families pay, but the tax code is also highly progressive among high earners because rates continue to rise. In 2006, the top 35 percent rate kicked in at $336,550, which is above the threshold for a family of four to qualify for the top 5 percent of earners. As taxpayers move into higher income brackets, they lose the ability to take certain deductions, and the alternative minimum tax (AMT) reduces the value of other deductions.

A family of four that earned enough to be in the top 1 percent of all income earners made $664,600 in 2006 and paid an effective income tax rate of 19 percent. Its tax bill for the year was $126,274.

A family that made enough to qualify for the top 5 percent of income earners made $268,800 and paid an effective income tax rate of 17.5 percent. Its tax bill was $47,040.

The family in the top 1 percent earned 147 percent more than the family in the top 5 percent but paid 168 percent more in taxes.

The difference is even larger when comparing a family in the top 10 percent to the family in the top 1 percent. A family in the top 10 percent earned $196,200 in 2006 and paid $31,392 in taxes for an effective income tax rate of 16 percent. The family in the top 1 percent earned 239 percent more than this family—and paid more than 300 percent more in taxes.

The Harm to Economic Growth

Progressive taxation dampens economic growth because it lessens the incentives of investors, savers, and entrepreneurs to take on new risk and reduces incentives for workers to put in longer hours. People work longer hours and extra days to earn additional income, and progressive taxation means they keep less of what they earn as their income rises. Not surprisingly, many workers decide that the extra effort is not worth it.

Savers and investors forgo spending their income today for the chance to earn high returns in the future, but progressive taxation means that as their returns increase, they pay higher tax rates and their after-tax returns decline. This makes spending their income now more attractive, and both investment and savings decline.

The risks of starting a new business are high, but the rewards often outweigh those risks—and not just for entrepreneurs. Workers and the economy as a whole benefit when entrepreneurs take on new risk, because the small businesses they create provide jobs for millions of Americans and often grow into larger businesses that create even more jobs.

Small businesses rely heavily on the profits they earn in the early stages of their development to fund growth and expansion. Progressivity takes more and more of these much-needed profits as businesses grow. This creates an entry barrier for many would-be entrepreneurs, discouraging many of them from taking risks to bring their ideas to market.

A Flatter Tax System

Even though the tax code is already steeply progressive, President Obama proposed in his budget, and Congress adopted in its budget resolution, a measure to make it even more punitive by raising the income tax rates for couples earning over $250,000 a year ($200,000 for singles) back to levels that applied before the 2001 and 2003 tax cuts. Under this plan, the top two rates will be 36 percent and 39.6 percent, compared to today's 33 percent and 35 percent.

To avoid increasing the damage that tax progressivity has already done to the economy, Congress should:

- Abandon the plan to raise tax rates on top earners and extend the 2001 and 2003 tax cuts for all taxpayers, and

- Reduce the progressivity of the tax code by eliminating several brackets and lowering the rates on those that remain.

Congress should aim for a tax code that treats taxpayers more equally: one that more closely resembles a flat tax. A tax code that has fewer tax brackets and lower rates would not punish success as a progressive taxation scheme does. It would tax all income similarly, so there would be no impediment to earning more.

Under a flatter tax system, those who earn more income still pay more taxes than those who earn less, but that difference will be more proportional to income. Under a flat tax that taxes all income at one rate, a family that earned 100 percent more than another family would pay 100 percent more in taxes—not nearly 1,000 percent more, as is the case under the current tax code.

Increasing the progressivity of the tax code threatens to further stifle economic growth. A code more in line with the flat tax is necessary to remove the barriers that block entrepreneurship and innovation. Regrettably, President Obama and Congress have chosen to follow liberal orthodoxy and put up more road blocks to economic growth by increasing the progressivity of the tax code through higher rates on top earners. They should look to the flat tax for inspiration instead.

Periodical Bibliography

The following articles have been selected to supplement the diverse views presented in this chapter.

William Ahern   "Can Income Tax Hikes Close the Deficit?" *Fiscal Facts No. 217*, March 12, 2010.

Neal Boortz   "The FairTax—The Truth," Townhall.com, November 27, 2007.

Sam Brownback   "The Optional Flat Tax," RealClearPolitics.com, July 19, 2007.

Duncan Currie   "America Has a Highly Progressive Tax System," *American*, October 24, 2008.

Ezra Klein   "Huckabee's Magic FairTax," *American Prospect Online*, January 17, 2008.

Robert Kuttner   "The Simplification Dodge," *American Prospect Online*, March 24, 2008.

Daniel J. Mitchell   "The Global Flat Tax Revolution: Lessons for Policy Makers," *Prosperitas*, February 2008.

Holley Ulbrich   "Flat Tax Is Class Warfare," *U.S. News & World Report*, April 12, 2010.

Laurence M. Vance   "The Flat Tax: The Answer to a Messy Code or Another Failed Approach?" *Atlanta Life*, October 2008.

Laurence M. Vance   "Can a Tax Be 'Fair'?" Campaign for Liberty, April 15, 2010.

For Further Discussion

Chapter 1

1. Doug Bandow argues that Americans are overtaxed. What would Michael Linden and Michael Ettlinger say to Bandow in response to his argument that the benefits received from taxes do not justify the amount of taxes paid?

2. Roberton Williams and Rosanne Altshuler claim there are five common myths about the US tax system. Name at least two instances elsewhere in this chapter where an author of a viewpoint perpetuates what Williams and Altshuler would call a myth.

Chapter 2

1. Both Robert Parry and Curtis S. Dubay mention the recent recession in their viewpoints. In what distinct ways do they each use the recession in their arguments for or against taxing the rich?

2. The National Center for Policy Analysis claims that tax cuts for the rich benefit both rich and poor. According to Chuck Marr and Gillian Brunet, what specific example disputes the claim that tax cuts for the rich are beneficial for all?

3. Leonard E. Burman notes that nearly all Americans pay some taxes in the form of Social Security and Medicare. Why does Ari Fleischer contend that the fact that low-income workers pay these taxes does not resolve the issue of fairness?

Chapter 3

1. Aviva Aron-Dine argues it is a myth that the Alternative Minimum Tax, or AMT, is becoming a middle-class tax.

Does Chris Edwards's argument for repeal depend upon the premise that the AMT is affecting the middle class?

2. Clive Crook argues in favor of a value-added tax, or VAT, whereas Daniel J. Mitchell argues against the VAT. Both agree that government spending requires additional money, but on what point do they disagree?

3. Americans for a Fair Estate Tax contend that it is fair that wealthy families pay an estate tax to contribute to the common good. What argument does Arthur B. Laffer give against the view that those lucky enough to inherit wealth should not have a portion of their inheritance redistributed?

Chapter 4

1. Holley Ulbrich argues that the simplicity of the flat tax is not a good reason to adopt it. To what extent does Daniel J. Mitchell appeal to the simplicity of the flat tax in support of it? What is his main argument in favor of the flat tax?

2. Given the discussion of progressivity by both Robin Blackburn and Curtis S. Dubay, which of the proposals in this chapter qualify as progressive and which do not? Justify your answer using textual support from either Blackburn or Dubay.

Organizations to Contact

The editors have compiled the following list of organizations concerned with the issues debated in this book. The descriptions are derived from materials provided by the organizations. All have publications or information available for interested readers. The list was compiled on the date of publication of the present volume; the information provided here may change. Be aware that many organizations take several weeks or longer to respond to inquiries, so allow as much time as possible.

American Enterprise Institute for Public Policy Research (AEI)
1150 Seventeenth St. NW, Washington, DC   20036
(202) 862-5800 • fax: (202) 862-7177
e-mail: info@aei.org
website: www.aei.org

The American Enterprise Institute for Public Policy Research is a private, nonpartisan, nonprofit institution dedicated to research and education on issues of government, politics, economics, and social welfare. AEI sponsors research and publishes materials focused on defending the principles and improving the institutions of American freedom and democratic capitalism. AEI publishes *The American*, a bimonthly magazine that often discusses tax policy.

Americans for Fair Taxation
3900 Essex Lane, Suite 328, Houston, TX   77027
(713) 963-9023 • fax: (713) 963-8403
e-mail: info@fairtax.org
website: www.fairtax.org

Americans for Fair Taxation is a nonprofit, nonpartisan, grassroots organization solely dedicated to replacing the current tax system. The organization developed the "FairTax" plan and works to implement the plan as a reform to the current US tax system. Americans for Fair Taxation produces numerous research papers available on its website, including "The Fair-Tax Reduces Complexity, Compliance Costs, and Noncompliance."

Brookings Institution

1775 Massachusetts Ave. NW, Washington, DC   20036
(202) 797-6000
e-mail: communications@brookings.edu
website: www.brookings.edu

The Brookings Institution is a nonprofit public policy organization that conducts independent research. The Urban-Brookings Tax Policy Center, a joint venture of the Urban Institute and Brookings Institution, provides analysis and facts about tax policy to policymakers, journalists, citizens, and researchers. The Urban-Brookings Tax Policy Center publishes many research reports and policy briefs, including "The Debate over Expiring Tax Cuts: What About the Deficit?"

Cato Institute

1000 Massachusetts Ave. NW, Washington, DC   20001
(202) 842-0200 • fax: (202) 842-3490
website: www.cato.org

The Cato Institute is a public policy research foundation dedicated to limiting the role of government, protecting individual liberties, and promoting free markets. The Cato Institute's economic research explores the benefits of lower taxes, a significantly reduced federal budget, and less government involvement in market processes. Among the organization's publications is the study, "Will Obama Raise Middle-Class Taxes to Fund Health Care?"

Center for American Progress

1333 H St. NW, 10th Floor, Washington, DC   20005
(202) 682-1611 • fax: (202) 682-1867
website: www.americanprogress.org

The Center for American Progress is a nonprofit, nonpartisan organization dedicated to improving the lives of Americans through progressive ideas and action. The Center for American Progress talks with leaders, thinkers, and citizens to explore the vital issues facing America and the world. The Center for American Progress publishes numerous research papers, which are available on its website, including "Audit the Tax Code: Doing What Works for Tax Expenditures."

Center for Freedom and Prosperity
PO Box 10882, Alexandria, VA   22310-9998
(202) 285-0244
e-mail: info@freedomandprosperity.org
website: www.freedomandprosperity.org

The Center for Freedom and Prosperity is a nonprofit organization created to lobby lawmakers in favor of market liberalization. The Center for Freedom and Prosperity Foundation is a nonprofit educational organization that publishes studies and conducts seminars analyzing the benefits of jurisdictional tax competition, financial privacy, and fiscal sovereignty. The Center for Freedom and Prosperity Foundation publishes the *Prosperitas* study series, which includes the recent article, "The Global Flat Tax Revolution: Lessons for Policy Makers."

Center on Budget and Policy Priorities (CBPP)
820 First St. NE, Suite 510, Washington, DC   20002
(202) 408-1080 • fax: (202) 408-1056
e-mail: center@cbpp.org
website: www.cbpp.org

The Center on Budget and Policy Priorities is a policy organization working at the federal and state levels on fiscal policy and public programs that affect low- and moderate-income families and individuals. The center conducts research and analysis to inform public debates about proposed budget and tax policies, and to help ensure that the needs of low-income families and individuals are considered in these debates. There are many reports available on the organization's website, including "High-Income People Would Benefit Significantly from Extension of 'Middle-Class' Tax Cuts."

Citizens for Tax Justice (CTJ)

1616 P St. NW, Suite 200, Washington, DC   20036
(202) 299-1066 • fax: (202) 299-1065
e-mail: ctj@ctj.org
website: www.ctj.org

Citizens for Tax Justice is a public interest research and advocacy organization focusing on the impact of federal, state, and local tax policies. CTJ fights for fair taxes for middle and low-income families, requiring the wealthy to pay their fair share, and closing corporate tax loopholes. CTJ publishes numerous reports, including "Latest State-by-State Estate Tax Data Show Why We Need a Strong Estate Tax."

Economic Policy Institute (EPI)

1333 H St. NW, Suite 300, East Tower
Washington, DC   20005-4707
(202) 775-8810 • fax: (202) 775-0819
e-mail: epi@epi.org
website: www.epi.org

The Economic Policy Institute is a nonprofit think tank that seeks to broaden the discussion about economic policy to include the interests of low- and middle-income workers. EPI briefs policymakers at all levels of government; provides technical support to national, state, and local activists and community organizations; testifies before national, state, and local legislatures; and provides information and background to the print and electronic media. EPI publishes books, studies, issue briefs, popular education materials, and other publications, among which is the biennially published *State of Working America*.

Institute for Research on the Economics of Taxation (IRET)

1710 Rhode Island Ave. NW, 11th Floor
Washington, DC 20036
(202) 463-1400 • fax: (202) 463-6199
e-mail: callen@iret.org
website: www.iret.org

The Institute for Research on the Economics of Taxation is a public policy research organization dedicated to the belief that constructive, free-market economic policies are essential for the nation's economic progress. IRET conducts research and analysis of the economic effects of tax, budget, and regulatory public policy initiatives, offering guidance to policymakers. IRET publishes frequent congressional advisories, including "Health Bills' Tax Increases Would Harm Health Care and the Economy."

National Taxpayers Union (NTU)

108 N Alfred St., Alexandria, VA 22314
(703) 683-5700 • fax: (703) 683-5722
e-mail: ntu@ntu.org
website: www.ntu.org

The National Taxpayers Union is a nonprofit, nonpartisan citizen organization working for lower taxes and smaller government at all levels. NTU aims to mobilize elected officials and the general public on behalf of tax relief and reform, lower and less wasteful spending, individual liberty, and free enterprise. NTU publishes news and action alerts on its website, as well as articles about tax basics, such as "Is the Income Tax Truly Voluntary?"

Tax Foundation

National Press Building, 529 14th St. NW, Suite 420
Washington, DC 20045-1000
(202) 464-6200
e-mail: tf@taxfoundation.org
website: www.taxfoundation.org

The Tax Foundation is a nonpartisan educational organization working to educate taxpayers about sound tax policy and the size of the tax burden borne by Americans. The Tax Foundation aims to gather data and publish information about the public sector in an objective, unbiased fashion. The Tax Foundation publishes *Fiscal Facts*, background papers, and special reports, such as "Tax Reform: Flat Tax or FairTax?"

United for a Fair Economy (UFE)
29 Winter St., Boston, MA   02108
(617) 423-2148 • fax: (617) 423-0191
e-mail: info@faireconomy.org
website: www.faireconomy.org

United for a Fair Economy is a movement support organization that works to narrow the gap between the wealthy and everyone else. UFE provides media capacity, face-to-face economic literacy education, and training resources to organizations and individuals who work to address the widening income and asset gaps in America. UFE provides overviews of issues and links to resources on its website. The organization also publishes several newsletters, including *Fair Play, Responsible Wealth Action News* and *Tax Fairness Action News.*

Urban Institute
2100 M St. NW, Washington, DC   20037
(202) 833-7200
website: www.urban.org

The Urban Institute works to foster sound public policy and effective government by gathering data, conducting research, evaluating programs, offering technical assistance overseas, and educating Americans about social and economic issues. The Urban-Brookings Tax Policy Center, a joint venture of the Urban Institute and Brookings Institution, provides analysis and facts about tax policy to policymakers, journalists, citizens, and researchers. The Urban-Brookings Tax Policy Center publishes many research reports and policy briefs, including "Extending Tax Credits for Low-Income Families."

Bibliography of Books

Henry J. Aaron and Leonard E. Burman — *Using Taxes to Reform Health Insurance: Pitfalls and Promises.* Washington, DC: Brookings Institution Press, 2008.

Mimi Abramovitz and Sandra Morgen — *Taxes Are a Woman's Issue: Reframing the Debate.* New York: Feminist Press at the City University of New York, 2006.

James Alm, Jorge Martinez-Vazquez, and Mark Rider, eds. — *The Challenges of Tax Reform in a Global Economy.* New York: Springer, 2006.

Alan J. Auerbach and Kevin A. Hassett, eds. — *Toward Fundamental Tax Reform.* Washington, DC: AEI Press, 2005.

Neal Boortz and John Linder — *The FairTax Book: Saying Goodbye to the Income Tax and the IRS.* New York: Regan Books, 2005.

Neal Boortz and John Linder, with Rob Woodall — *FairTax, the Truth: Answering the Critics.* New York: Harper, 2008.

David F. Bradford — *The X-Tax in the World Economy: Going Global with a Simple, Progressive Tax.* Washington, DC: AEI Press, 2004.

Leslie Carbone — *Slaying Leviathan: The Moral Case for Tax Reform.* Washington, DC: Potomac Books, 2009.

John W. Diamond
and George R.
Zodrow, eds.

Fundamental Tax Reform: Issues, Choices, and Implications. Cambridge, MA: MIT Press, 2008.

Chris Edwards
and Daniel J.
Mitchell

Global Tax Revolution: The Rise of Tax Competition and the Battle to Defend It. Washington, DC: Cato Institute, 2008.

Steve Forbes

Flat Tax Revolution: Using a Postcard to Abolish the IRS. Washington, DC: Regnery Publishing, 2005.

Michael J. Graetz

100 Million Unnecessary Returns: A Simple, Fair, and Competitive Tax Plan for the United States. New Haven, CT: Yale University Press, 2010.

Michael J. Graetz
and Ian Shapiro

Death by a Thousand Cuts: The Fight Over Taxing Inherited Wealth. Princeton, NJ: Princeton University Press, 2006.

Michael S. Greve

Sell Globally, Tax Locally: Sales Tax Reform for the New Economy. Washington, DC: AEI Press, 2003.

David Cay
Johnston

Perfectly Legal: The Covert Campaign to Rig Our Tax System to Benefit the Super Rich—and Cheat Everybody Else. New York: Portfolio, 2003.

James John
Jurinski

Tax Reform: A Reference Handbook. Santa Barbara, CA: ABC-CLIO, 2000.

Edward J.
McCaffery

Fair Not Flat: How to Make the Tax System Better and Simpler. Chicago, IL: University of Chicago Press, 2002.

Benjamin I. Page and Lawrence R. Jacobs   *Class War? What Americans Really Think About Economic Inequality.* Chicago, IL: University of Chicago Press, 2009.

Peter Saunders, ed.   *Taxploitation: The Case for Income Tax Reform.* St. Leonards, N.S.W.: Centre for Independent Studies, 2006.

Alan Schenk and Oliver Oldman   *Value Added Tax: A Comparative Approach.* New York: Cambridge University Press, 2007.

Daniel N. Shaviro   *Corporate Tax Shelters in a Global Economy: Why They Are a Problem and What We Can Do About It.* Washington, DC: AEI Press, 2004.

Joel Slemrod and Jon Bakija   *Taxing Ourselves: A Citizen's Guide to the Debate Over Taxes,* 4th ed. Cambridge, MA: MIT Press, 2008.

C. Eugene Steuerle   *Contemporary U.S. Tax Policy,* 2nd ed. Washington, DC: Urban Institute Press, 2008.

Alan D. Viard, ed.   *Tax Policy Lessons from the 2000s.* Washington, DC: AEI Press, 2009.

George R. Zodrow and Peter Mieszkowski, eds.   *United States Tax Reform in the 21st Century.* New York: Cambridge University Press, 2002.

Index